Falling short?

The *Alpha* Course examined

Chris Hand

© Day One Publications 1998
First printed 1998

Scripture quotations are from The New King James Version.
© 1982 Thomas Nelson Inc.

British Library Cataloguing in Publication Data available
ISBN 0 902548 88 3

Published by Day One Publications
3 Epsom Business Park, Kiln Lane, Epsom, Surrey KT17 1JF.
☎ 01372 728 300 **FAX** 01372 722 400
e-mail address: ldos.dayone@ukonline.co.uk

Designed by Steve Devane. Production services by Indeprint Ltd.
Printed by Bell and Bain Ltd Glasgow

Contents

The question is being repeatedly asked: has anyone written an appraisal of the *Alpha* Course? *Alpha* has been enthusiastically taken up by numerous churches as a method of evangelism. Its compilers stress that it combines the informality of home surroundings with a cutting down of the Gospel to absolute 'Basics'. Many pastors, however, have voiced their strong concern about a perceived distortion of Gospel teaching. Others murmur that it is a Trojan horse designed to achieve greater charismatic penetration of 'traditional' churches. (It certainly comes from the same stable as the Toronto Blessing, and brings participants very quickly to learn a charismatic view of the Holy Spirit.)

The methods and content of the *Alpha* Course represent a radically different handling of the Gospel than that which evangelicals have employed in the past. The difference is so great, amounting to a startling new direction, that discerning Christians should weigh it with great caution.

A careful analysis is clearly overdue, 'careful' being the key word, because anything not fairly reasoned and documented can hardly be expected to stimulate serious thought.

This examination of the *Alpha* Course perfectly meets the need expressed by pastors and church leaders. It is a quality-critique, expertly drawing together background, content, and results. The view it provides of all aspects of the course will both shock and disturb those who count loyalty to the Bible as paramount.

Any ministry of warning risks misunderstanding in today's super-irenic culture. Yet wrong turnings in all ages take pilgrims far off course, and the author's pastoral concern is obvious. It is to urge his readers to keep closely to biblical methods in their witness to a lost world. May this volume go far and wide, stimulating God's people to seriously consider the issues at stake.

Dr Peter Masters
Metropolitan Tabernacle
London

M any friends have encouraged me along the way and helped shape my thinking, whether they realise it or not, to be able to approach a subject like this in the way that I have. I have been greatly helped by the ministry of the the London Reformed Baptist Seminary at the Metropolitan Tabernacle in London led by Dr Peter Masters. Good friends like Alan Morrison, Nick Needham and Alec Taylor have also played a big part in pointing me towards reformed understanding.

A special thank-you to Peter and Sara Glover whose friendship and encouragement has been particularly appreciated and often timely. Their practical help and the stimulating conversations that we had along the way have been invaluable. A big thank you to them. Also Alan Howe has helped greatly by his interest and insights.

My wife Caroline has provided great support, not least in her capacity as proof-reader and honest critic. Her influence has borne fruit in sharpening up and focussing parts of the argument of this book. I am grateful to her for all this and more.

John Roberts and Steve Devane at Day One have worked well in keeping things on track. I have been glad of their interest and support for this book.

Chris Hand
Lewisham
London

July 1998

Alpha: A modern day success story?

'Success stories' in the Christian world are few and far between. For most of us seeking to make known the name of Jesus Christ, the work of evangelism is hard in the West today. While blessed in the past with glorious days when the Lord moved in great power, those days are now a distant memory. Today few seem to want to listen to the claims of the gospel. Not many pause to hear of the Saviour of men who has done everything necessary for the salvation of souls from eternal destruction. Few, even when they stop to listen, are then converted. There have been wonderful exceptions. But the general rule remains. Success stories are in short supply.

It has come as a welcome surprise to many to discover an evangelistic tool that appears to have gone against the trend. The *Alpha* Course, a series of 15 Bible Studies designed to introduce people to the Christian faith and establish new converts in basic doctrine, has forced itself into the reckoning simply because of its huge apparent success. With its well-designed logo and 'ready-to-use' format, many churches have been greatly impressed with its seeming ability to communicate the gospel effectively to today's generation. People are wondering whether they should perhaps bring *Alpha* into their own churches as a way of boosting their evangelistic results. Some who might not agree with all the emphases of *Alpha* are anxious not to miss out on something the Lord may be blessing. It is a big issue. What are we to make of the *Alpha* course?

What's happening on the ground?
Alpha's seeming fruitfulness in converting people has been so remarkable that in many churches it is now the mainstay of their evangelistic endeavours. Stories abound as to the success that it has brought. Some churches which had flagged in their outreach programmes have found fresh inspiration by embracing it and attribute much of the blessing their church has received to the use they have made of this evangelistic course. Typical

among the comments from pastors and leaders who are using *Alpha* in their churches is the following:

As we draw to the end of our fourth Alpha, it becomes increasingly difficult to put into words what we see God doing. It is such a thrill to see every single person, including leaders and helpers, touched and changed by the Holy Spirit. It is simply beyond human belief. (Alpha News July 1996, P9)

Reports abound as to the transformation *Alpha* has brought to relationships within churches as people have learned to work together. Believers have been reinvigorated with a zeal to reach the lost. The following comment is typical:

Alpha has had a profound effect on the lives of the people at our church. Over 100 people have been involved and this has had quite a unifying effect on the church. It's as though, suddenly, everyone has started pulling on the oars at the same time and in the same direction. It has given a common purpose and momentum to our ministry and mission and taken us away from an increasingly dangerous state of introversion. (Alpha News November 1996, P8)

Most important of all, it has, according to many witnesses, established itself with a proven track record of being able to draw in unbelievers and seemingly convert them. One user of *Alpha* reports his satisfaction with the course:

This evangelist can confidently say that it is the most effective form of evangelism and nurture he's ever experienced and anyone can do it. I won't pretend that Alpha is easy—it's been a hard slog, but the Lord is using the church's efforts throughout the UK and beyond to reap a great harvest. (Alpha News November 1996, P8)

This is just one example. Many others believe they are witnessing the same evangelistic success and seeing an unprecedented number of conversions.

It's everywhere!

It has to be said that *Alpha's* growth and popularity have been nothing short of staggering. Beginning as a 'within-house' evangelistic and discipling tool at Holy Trinity Brompton, (HTB), a large and thriving charismatic Anglican church in west London, its progress has taken it far beyond the confines of the UK. As this book is being written, the course is being run in Albania, Bolivia, Finland, Serbia, Namibia, Kenya, Switzerland and South Korea, and that is to name but a few countries. There is every reason to suppose that the current list will soon be outdated, such has been its meteoric rise to prominence and acceptance in the evangelical church.

Using statistics published by HTB in their regular bulletin, 'Alpha News', a conservative estimate of churches conducting the course was put at more than 200 at the end of 1993 (*Alpha News* December 1993, P1). By April 1994, the number of participating churches and Christian groups was over 400 (*Alpha News* April 1994, P1). By April 1995, it had reached 1200 (*Alpha News* April 1995, P1) and a year later in July 1996 it had leapt to 4000 worldwide (*Alpha News* July 1996, P1). The most recent figure puts the number of courses at 7500 (*Alpha News* March 1998, P1). Estimates of the number of **people** who had done *Alpha* run as follows:

1991	600
1992	1000
1993	4500
1994	30,000
1995	100,000
1996	250,000
1997	500,000

(*Alpha News* February 1997, P1)

Even allowing for some over-reporting, it is highly likely that these figures **underestimate** the number of people participating since not all churches register. From whatever angle one looks at it, the impact of *Alpha* is literally world-wide.

Events are periodically organised in order to raise the profile of the course and guarantee its continued expansion. An '*Alpha* National

Weekend' was held on 13-14 January 1996 when more than 45 bookshops promoted the *Alpha* materials simultaneously with 30 *Alpha* training courses, whilst 250 churches held special guest services to promote the course (*Alpha News* March 1996, P4). National media campaigns in the UK have also been planned, and a general mobilisation of participating churches has been called for in order to advertise *Alpha* throughout the nation. *Alpha News* is used to show the growth and development of the course, to report testimonies and convey any favourable comment that can be garnered from church leaders and theologians. Posters, sweatshirts, T-shirts and car stickers are available, as well as videos of the course itself and manuals for leaders. Training days are regularly held for those who want to know about the course and how to hold *Alpha* in their own churches.

What do the 'experts' say about Alpha?

Alpha has not been without some very well-known champions and supporters. Each copy of the *Alpha News* lists these. Among those who have endorsed the course are:

George Carey, the Archbishop of Canterbury
David Hope, the Archbishop of York
Alistair McGrath of Wycliffe Hall, Oxford and Regent College, Vancouver
Luis Palau, international evangelist
J.I. Packer of Regent College, Vancouver.
The late John Wimber of the Association of Vineyard Churches
R.T. Kendall of Westminster Chapel
Joel Edwards of the Evangelical Alliance

This is just a representative sample. Two whole pages of *Alpha News* are sometimes given over purely to the comments of church leaders. Denominations that support *Alpha* include Anglican, Methodist, Baptist, Roman Catholic and 'new churches'. Why do so many lend their weight to the course? Because:

a) It works!
This appears to be the main reason that is cited.

We find for example, John James, President of the Baptist Union, speaking well of the course in these words:

I commend the Alpha course because I know that many hundreds of our Baptist Churches are finding it very helpful in reaching rank outsiders to the local church. (Alpha News February 1997, P29)

Steve Chalke of Oasis Trust agrees with this:

Alpha is the most effective and transferable introductory course to the Christian faith that I know. (Alpha News February 1997, P29)

Quite simply, people believe *Alpha* works.

b) A tool for our day
Others have been impressed by the seeming ability of the course to communicate with today's culture. Rev Canon Robert Warren, National Officer for Evangelism, remarks:

One of the most significant developments in evangelism in recent years. Alpha is a proven, thoroughly tested, well researched, marvellously presented way of communicating the gospel in today's culture. (Alpha News February 1997, P29)

This was the late John Wimber's view as well.

Alpha is ingenuous in the way that it brings people into a private setting by invitation. So you are accommodating the 20th Century culture in a very manageable and functional way and I am thrilled with it. (Alpha News February 1997, P29)

The 'relevance issue' is felt then by many to be one of the main advantages with *Alpha*. It has something to say which will be heard by people living in the post-modern world at the end of the twentieth century.

c) It's cringe-free!
Another benefit people feel about *Alpha* is its ability to bring non-

Christians under the sound of the gospel without them feeling threatened. The use of a meal beforehand, the 'low-key' approach, and the employment of humour make this possible along with the openness to questions and the important part that interaction in small groups plays. This impressed Joel Edwards, Director General of the Evangelical Alliance:

The great command to make disciples of all people is still relevant today. Alpha provides us with a contemporary response to cringe free evangelism which deserves the increasing profile it is currently receiving. (Alpha News February 1997, P29)

Fiona Castle remarks,

I am delighted to commend the Alpha course as a totally non-threatening yet challenging way of presenting the gospel. (Alpha News February 1997, P29)

Gerald Coates takes this further still by saying, *'The course is fun and unthreatening–just like our Lord Himself!' (Alpha News February 1997, P29)* The strength of the course lies then, for some at least, in the fact that it avoids the 'threatening' approach of other evangelistic methods and avoids making people 'cringe'.

Taking a second look

This book would not be necessary if everything that has been so far written could be taken at face value. Any Bible-believing Christian with a concern to reach this unbelieving world would be delighted to know of a course that was seeing the regular success which the *Alpha* course is claiming. Its published statistics would be allowed to tell their own story and this book could have finished here with a hearty recommendation to start an *Alpha* course in every church in the land as soon as possible.

But there are questions that do have to be asked. Are we hearing the whole story? Are there details that we are missing and which would put things in a different light? Does the *Alpha* course actually achieve the success which its users and supporters make out for it? How does it actually work? And perhaps the most important question of all, is *Alpha* an authentic presentation of the gospel? Does it really communicate the truths of the gospel?

What's the big deal?

It is important to ask and try to answer these questions for a whole variety of reasons. One of these is that Christians, like anybody else, are easily swayed. The herd mentality can easily take over and lead us to accept things that we should really reject. In this day of 'small things' we are also very susceptible to uncritically receive something new in our churches simply because it appears to 'work'. At times of such difficulty and disappointment in preaching the gospel, it is a great temptation to clutch at straws and try anything that we have been told 'works'.

The Lord Himself warned us *'And because iniquity shall abound, the love of many shall wax cold. But he that shall endure unto the end, the same shall be saved.' (Matthew 24:12-13 KJV)*. Those words are true for us today when the Christian church is surrounded by the forces of secular thought, pluralistic culture and eastern/New Age philosophy. We have to be careful in case we are doing something for pragmatic reasons and against the rule of Scripture and our better judgement. In this day when so few churches see increase, it is very easy to try something out because 'it works' rather than assessing it properly.

In introducing *Alpha*, Sandy Millar, the vicar of HTB, tells us that in the course:

The issues are clearly put and the claims of Christ examined—all in the company of other searchers in an atmosphere of love and acceptance. By taking account of literally thousands of questionnaires, the Alpha course has been adapted and improved so it is truly moulded to the perceived and experienced needs of this generation. Stripping the gospel down to its bare essentials, it makes Christianity accessible to men and women of today's culture. (Alpha News April 1995, P2)

But what are these 'bare essentials'? What is left out? What is left in? Which doctrines are thought essential and which are not? Which 'claims of Christ' are being considered and how clearly does it fit within any recognisable example of New Testament preaching and gospel presentation?

It is of the utmost importance that we are clear in our understanding of what the gospel is. A brief moment's thought will confirm the importance of this. We owe it after all to the people who are doing the course. If the success of *Alpha* is spurious, it means that currently there are many people under the illusion that they have become Christians when the likelihood is that they have not. Of all the illusions to labour under, this ranks as perhaps the worst imaginable. Such a terrible scenario does not come from the imagination of man. It comes from the words of Scripture. It is possible to appear religious yet still be without saving knowledge of Christ. It is within the realms of possibility to say 'Lord, Lord' and yet hear the words from the King of Glory *'I never knew you; depart from Me, you who practise lawlessness! (Matthew 7:23).* We need to ensure that we are not among those shouldering some of the responsibility for such spurious converts.

But we also owe it to the church of Christ to look more closely. For the well-being of the church is also at stake. Again it only takes a moment's reflection to realise the implications. What would the effect be on the future of the church if large numbers of unconverted people swelled its ranks? It would of course be catastrophic. The presence of unconverted people, some of whom would subsequently reach positions of power and authority, would be ruinous for the health of the church. If the work of evangelism is poorly or mistakenly conducted, we court the risk of failing the Apostle Paul's injunctions in 1 Corinthians 3 regarding Christian ministry:

According to the grace of God which was given to me, as a wise masterbuilder I have laid the foundation, and another builds on it. But let each one take heed how he builds on it. For no other foundation can anyone lay than that which is laid, which is Jesus Christ. Now if anyone builds on this foundation with gold, silver, precious stones, wood, hay, straw, each one's work will become clear; for the Day will declare it, because it will be revealed by fire; and the fire will test each one's work, of what sort it is. (1 Corinthians 3:10-13)

Many denominations across the world today bear the marks of what happens when unconverted people ascend to prominence and exert influence. If 'wood, hay and straw' are being brought into the church instead of 'gold, silver and precious stones', it will be a poorer building for it and will not withstand the scrutiny of the Master. How evangelism is conducted is of paramount importance, and failure to follow biblical principles will lead to untold disaster in the professing church. For these and other reasons, we have to take a closer look at *Alpha* and subject its claims to closer examination.

Where do we go from here?

The next task is to take a brief look at the *Alpha* course itself. What topics does it cover? How does the course actually work? Chapter Two tackles this issue. It will not be an exhaustive description but will serve to give a general idea of the course content.

After this, we will be asking a very basic question–what is the gospel? This is a vital question to ask. If *Alpha* fails to present the gospel, then it fails to qualify as an evangelistic tool. It is as simple as that. Chapters Three and Four will attempt to outline at length what the gospel is. What truths does it communicate? How does it communicate them? What demands does it make of us? To find our answers we shall mostly be looking in the Acts of the Apostles.

Chapter Five details the evangelistic material used on the *Alpha* course. An evaluation of *Alpha* as an evangelistic tool is the main focus of this book. The evangelistic material therefore has to be described carefully, as this forms the basis for the following two chapters which examine the gospel preached in the *Alpha* course and compare it with that found in Scripture. Here we will see how successful *Alpha* has been in presenting the gospel 'stripped down to its bare essentials'. Chapter Eight follows this up with an examination of the experiences that people report and in particular the part played by the 'Weekend Away'. Do the experiences which people have correlate with conversion? Are there, for example, indications that true repentance and faith are present? Or is something else entirely different happening?

Chapter Nine raises some further concerns about the definition of what a Christian is. How does *Alpha* understand this? We then draw some final conclusions.

Alpha: What is it?

The foundations of the *Alpha* course were originally laid in 1979 through the work of Charles Marnham (Gumbel 1997a, P17). During his time at Holy Trinity Brompton, (HTB), in west London, he sought to devise a course to look at the basics of the Christian faith in a way that would be helpful to new Christians.

After Marnham's initial input, *Alpha* gradually evolved. One of the key figures in this and the main architect of the *Alpha* course as it now exists is Nicky Gumbel, currently curate at HTB. Indeed it was through Gumbel's vision and work that *Alpha* grew to have the impact it has today.

What is the Alpha Course?

Alpha is really quite straightforward in terms of its concept and design. It is a series of 15 talks given over a period of ten weeks. The talks are on set topics and these can be delivered either by a speaker or by using specially produced videos or tapes. It is reported that two thirds of participating churches use the videos to present the *Alpha* course. These videos are based upon a book entitled '*Questions of Life*' which is the basic text book for the course and sets out the structure and content of *Alpha*.

Typically each talk takes place on a weekday evening and is preceded by a supper provided by church members for people who have been invited to attend the course. Taking as a model the system used at HTB, the supper is followed by some notices and perhaps a short time of worship. The main talk lasts about 45 minutes after which coffee and biscuits are served. Then people go into groups of about 12 to discuss issues raised in the talk and to ask questions. These groups are led by church members, although non-Christians may be employed as helpers in these groups (Gumbel 1997a, P0). A great premium is put upon interaction and the whole environment is meant to enable people to ask whatever questions they have without feeling embarrassed. There are leadership manuals for those group leaders as well as course books for those participating.

The Structure and Content of Alpha

The order in which some of the lessons occur may vary. The 'Weekend Away', for example, may take place at a different point. Nevertheless the following order sketches out the typical way the course unfolds.

a) Lessons 1-3 : The evangelistic element

The evangelistic part of the course is dealt with during the first three weeks. Just a brief outline is given here as this subject matter is looked at in more detail in Chapter Five.

When *Alpha* works as it is intended, the first week is a supper at which the topic *'Christianity: Boring, Untrue and Irrelevant?'* is examined. It sets the tone for what follows. For the most part it is a description of the ills of the modern world and modern man's search for meaning. At the conclusion of it, the leader *'...then invites people to join the next Alpha course'* (*Alpha News July 1996, P14*).

Lesson One also fulfils another function because it is not only the beginning but also the end-point of the course. For people completing the course it is described as an opportunity to 'celebrate' (*Alpha News, July 1996, P14*). The idea is, however, that they bring with them some friends or family who will then enlist for the next *Alpha* course. In this way, through people introducing friends to the course, *Alpha* perpetuates itself and can be run on a continuous basis, which is what many churches do. In effect, people attend Lesson One twice—once at the beginning of the course when they are brought as guests and then again at the end of the course to 'celebrate' and to bring their own guests in turn.

After this introductory session, Lesson Two deals with the issue *'Who is Jesus?'* and looks at the factual evidence for His life and for His claims to be God. As with most of the topics, the material is well supported with Biblical quotations. The case for the historical and literal resurrection of the Lord is strongly put and there is also evidence drawn from a variety of sources to establish the truthfulness of the biblical witness.

The evangelistic thrust proper comes in the next lesson which is entitled *'Why did Jesus die?'*. This is the most important evangelistic lesson and we will therefore defer an examination of it until Chapter Five.

b) Lessons 4-7: Pastoral guidance
Everything in the course from here onwards presumes that the course participant has questions of a more or less practical nature that need answering. The assumption is that the person is a Christian and the questions are answered without any further use of evangelistic argument or reasoning.

In Week Four, the topic of assurance is dealt with under three main headings. These are:

★ **The Word of God**–the promise that if we 'open the door to the Lord', He will come and be with us (Gumbel 1997b, P60-63).
★ **The Work of Jesus**–the fact of Christ's death upon the cross assuring us that God has forgiven us (Gumbel 1997b, P63-66); and-
★ **The Witness of the Spirit**– the change in character that takes place in the person's life when converted along with the inner conviction that the person is now a child of God (Gumbel 1997b, P66-69).

Week Five tackles the issue of '*Why read the Bible?*'. Here topics such as the inspiration of Scripture are looked at and defended. The Bible is affirmed as the '...*supreme authority for what we believe and how we act..*' (*Gumbel 1997b, P78*) although *Alpha* does allow that, *God also speaks to people directly by his Spirit: through prophecy, dreams, visions, and through other people.* (Gumbel 1997b, P75).

This is an indication of *Alpha's* overtly charismatic content which becomes more pronounced as the course progresses. The Bible's role in setting rules and boundaries for us is stressed as is its function in drawing us into a closer relationship with the Lord. Some practical guidance is given as well as a description of the benefits of Bible study.

Week Six examines the matter of '*Why and how should we pray?*'. The role of the Trinity in prayer is set out and some objections to prayer are discussed. Again there is some practical guidance that is given and some lessons are drawn from the Lord's Prayer.

After this, attention turns to "*How does God guide us?*" , where again there are strongly charismatic overtones with reference to dreams (Gumbel 1997b, P112-113) and prophecy (Gumbel 1997b, P112).

c) Lessons 8-11: the Alpha 'Weekend Away'.
A key point is reached here, when people on the course are invited to go on a 'Weekend Away'. This is a vital component of the course and we will look at it in greater detail in Chapter Eight.

It basically sets out to answer the question *'What about the Holy Spirit?'.* This is done in three lessons:

★ **'Who is the Holy Spirit?'**–a theological study of the work of the Spirit from Old Testament times to Pentecost;
★ **'What does the Holy Spirit do?'**–the work of the Spirit to make the believer aware of his adoption into God's family and to mould him into the 'family likeness' of Christ, as well as the issue of spiritual gifts;
★ **'How can I be filled with the Spirit?'**–this describes the experiences associated with being 'filled with the Spirit' and the benefits to be derived.

The teaching on the Holy Spirit is typical of what is found in many Pentecostal/Charismatic churches today. This is one of the most obvious places where the charismatic nature of the course is explicitly emphasised.

The 'Weekend Away' often concludes with a topic called *'How can I make the most of the rest of my life?',* although on other occasions this topic is reserved until later in the course. Here, practical guidance is given about holiness and in particular for the need for godliness in relationships with members of the opposite sex.

d) Lessons 12-15: More pastoral and practical guidance
Lesson 12 looks at the question of *'How can I resist evil?'.* It affirms belief in the person of the devil and gives guidance as to how to combat him.

Lesson 13 takes up the theme of *'Why and how should we tell others?'* which once more contains some unremarkable material, but does have a charismatic element with its understanding of the role of power (Gumbel 1997b, P197-198) through healing and supernatural displays. Lesson 14 then poses the question *'Does God heal today?'.* In the introduction to this lesson, Nicky Gumbel relates how he advanced in his understanding of this matter following a visit by the late John Wimber, founder of the Vineyard Movement, a charismatic group from the USA. A 'supernatural' insight was shared that a woman present in the room was sterile. After prayer the woman was able to conceive (Gumbel 1997b, P203-204). Gumbel goes on to say:

I decided to reread the Bible to try to understand what it said about healing. The more I have looked, the more convinced I am that we should expect God to heal miraculously today. (Gumbel 1997B, P204)

He concludes the lesson with a particular anecdote which led to some people professing faith in Christ where '*They did so because they knew they had seen God's power in healing*' (Gumbel 1997b, P220).

The last formal session in the course ends on the question '*What about the church?*' with a defence of the need for attendance at church. As we shall see in Chapter Nine, its understanding of 'the church' is very broad.

Adapting *Alpha*

There have been various adaptations of the *Alpha* to fit different groups. There is, for example, *Youth Alpha* for young people. In February 1997 it was estimated that 270 churches were using this adaptation for young people (*Alpha News* February 1997, P9) with further courses being done in Christian Unions at schools.

Alpha courses have been run in prisons (*Alpha News* July 1997: 6-7) and at lunch-time meetings in places of work as well as broadcast on 'Christian Radio' in London (*Alpha News,* December 1995, P3). Of course, no two churches approach the material in exactly the same way. There is room for innovation and variations. The subject of water baptism, for example, may be included by those of a Baptist persuasion, the subject itself being absent from the *Alpha* course, although churches are not encouraged to teach doctrinal distinctives (Gumbel 1997a, P193). Similarly, it is not practicable for all churches to have a 'Weekend Away'. This is most obviously the case with courses held in prisons! But it is also relevant for other churches which would not have the resources to have a 'Weekend Away'. Instead there are adaptations so that a special day–perhaps a Saturday–could be held at the church to deal with the subject of the Holy Spirit. Alternatively, the 'Weekend Away' material might be condensed into shorter sessions that could be done in a morning at the church.

The course is flexible, but not too flexible. HTB has warned against imitations of *Alpha* which trade under the name but which do not contain some of the elements of *Alpha*. To combat the misuse of its titles and name, Sandy Millar, the vicar of HTB, has had to issue a statement to combat the confusion caused by courses run as *Alpha* courses but which failed to meet the criteria. He comments:

Now that Alpha is running all around the world we have reluctantly had to draw up a copyright statement more tightly in order to preserve confidence and quality control. (Alpha News, November 1996, P24)

As recorded in a statement dated 2 October 1996, minor adaptations are permitted as long as they are not marketed over an area wider than the local church concerned. These adaptations allow that:

...the Alpha course may be shortened or lengthened by varying the length of the talks or the number of sessions. Not all the material need be used; additional material may be used. (Alpha News, November 1996, P24)

But these changes are permitted subject to the following proviso: *Such alterations must not change* **the essential character of the course.**

Alpha is a series of about 15 talks, given over a period of time, including a weekend or day away, with teaching based on the material in 'Questions of Life'. (Alpha News, November 1996, P24 Emphasis in the original)

'*Questions of Life*' is the essence of *Alpha* and is the main place we look to understand the course content. The videos, for example, basically follow the structure of '*Questions of Life*'. No 'test case' of what constitutes the 'essential character' of *Alpha* has to date taken place, but it is evident from what follows that the teaching on the Holy Spirit at the 'Weekend/Day Away' is regarded as integral to the course. From what has already been described, any church that decided to involve itself in *Alpha* but wanted to 'opt out' of the charismatic part would drastically have to curtail some parts of the course including the 'Weekend Away'. Given the charismatic commitment of the course, such alterations would possibly fall foul of the requirement of the copyright statement!

As we have seen in this brief description, much of the *Alpha* course does not startle in its treatment of some subjects. It quotes from a variety of sources and is attractively presented. There are plenty of illustrations and quotations from Scripture. It is 'up front' about being charismatic and this is a feature that is very prominent. There is much more that could be said. Just the 'bare bones' have been set out here. We return to look at the evangelistic material and the 'Weekend Away' in more detail later, but our discussion now leads us to the central issue of the gospel.

Gospel truth

What is the gospel? It would be difficult to think of a more basic question. All Christians would agree on that. No gospel means no message. If the gospel is the '...*power of God to salvation for everyone who believes...' (Romans 1:16)*, it is obviously essential and its proclamation the most important task of the church.

In the light of the importance of the subject, it is curious that the answer to the question 'What is the gospel?' is assumed by some professing Christians to be straightforward and self-evident, indeed hardly worth a mention. Some popular books on evangelism more or less proceed with the assumption that we all know what we are talking about when we speak of the gospel and evangelism. Contemporary treatments of the subject concentrate more on the problems of adapting the message to the culture of those being addressed, or the problems of overcoming shyness and initiating conversations with unbelievers. It is simply assumed that we all know what the message is.

Let us consider what is at stake here. Go wrong on the gospel and all that follows will of necessity be flawed. Lose our way on the meaning of the gospel and we are on the fast track to losing what distinguishes true Christianity from anything else. So we shall be looking in this chapter briefly at the content of the gospel. It is a huge subject. Whether we are aware or not, it has generated many great and heated debates. But we shall have to confine ourselves to some basic issues. What does the gospel **say?** What **truths** does it **communicate** to us? Do we really know what we mean by the gospel? Then in the next chapter we will see how the gospel addresses us and what conditions it sets out.

Looking in Acts

An obvious place to look for answers to our questions is the book of Acts of the Apostles. The reason is quite simple. In Acts we have actual examples of gospel preaching for us to study. There are sermons preached by the apostles, albeit in summary form, to unconverted people, sometimes of Jewish origin, sometimes of Gentile extraction, sometimes a mixture of both, but with the same clear end in view—their conversion. In Acts we are privileged to be able to observe both the **messages** and **methods** of the apostles who were speaking, we must remember, under the inspiration of the Holy Spirit. Their words, therefore, are exactly as God intended them to be.

They convey His truth not only to the people who first heard them in Jerusalem, Athens, Lystra, or wherever it might have been, but also for future generations like ourselves. They are given to us so that we might learn and be able to carry out the task in the way that God intends. In the apostles we have men whose function was to lay the foundations upon which the ministry of the church of Jesus Christ is to be built.

In particular the sermon preached in Acts 17 to the mainly pagan audience in Athens will be the example that we will look at most carefully. Why use this sermon? It is because the Athens of Paul's day is perhaps the culture and context which comes closest to that of the present day. It most nearly approximates to our present society whose roots and moorings are increasingly divorced from the knowledge of God. The sermon to the people in Athens is given in a pagan culture to pagans. However much we might like to disguise the truth from ourselves in the West, that is essentially the context of our evangelism today.

We will also look at some of the teaching of the Lord Jesus Christ. He is the Evangelist without peer. It was he who looked upon the unbelieving generation of His day and declared:

O Jerusalem, Jerusalem, the one who kills the prophets and stones those who are sent to her! How often I wanted to gather your children together, as a hen gathers her chicks under her wings, but you were not willing! (Matthew 23:37)

The teaching of the Saviour, although unique in method, gives us invaluable lessons in the work of the gospel.

What is the Message of the Gospel?
There are many ways to try to understand the content of the gospel message. What information does it convey to us? What does it tell us? The analysis that follows is not definitive but highlights some key features.

a) The Gospel is about the God whom we do not know

The gospel is a message from God. It comes from Him and is essentially, revelation about Him. It has been given to mankind by Him, and without the gospel, we would be none the wiser about God or our standing before Him. Speaking to the Galatians, the apostle Paul informs them:

But I make known to you, brethren, that the gospel which was preached by me is not according to man. For I neither received it from man, nor was I taught it, but it came through the revelation of Jesus Christ. (Galatians 1:11-12)

In the light of the fact that the gospel comes from Him, it is not surprising to learn that He is the central focus of the message. It conveys to man facts about God's character, thoughts, desires and will. The gospel gives to us knowledge about God that we would not otherwise possess. Man comes into the frame only inasmuch as he relates to what God has shown about Himself. Thus we are told that the '...*wrath of God is revealed from heaven against all ungodliness and unrighteousness of men* ...*(Romans 1:18).* God tells us something about himself that is communicated to man by revelation from himself, 'from heaven.' By him similarly, '...*the righteousness of God apart from the law is revealed...' (Romans 3:21).* It is **his** wrath and **his** righteousness that is revealed. We occupy the place of people needing to have things shown to them. Man is incidental. God is central.

Turning to Acts 17 and Paul's sermon to the pagans in Athens, we find these same things emphasised. After making an observation about the people of the city and their religious observances (Acts 17:22), Paul seizes upon an inscription on an altar he has noted during his travels around the city that is consecrated 'TO THE UNKNOWN GOD' (Acts 17:23). Why does Paul do this? What does the inscription tell us? It informs us that man is chargeable with ignorance about the true and living God. He simply does not know Him. In the light of this ignorance Paul boldly declares '...*Him I proclaim to you' (Acts 17:23).*

And there we have it. It is so obvious that it is almost overlooked. The gospel must have at its heart an accurate portrait of God Himself. He must be described. We need to be told about Him, His character, His works and

His purposes. The gospel is a message from God that tells us what He is like.

b) God is the Creator and Sustainer of the world
So how does Paul proceed to describe this God to his audience? We might think for this pagan audience, full of philosophical scepticism and living with the uncertainties and fears generated by the unpredictable and irascible 'gods' they served, that there might be a message of comfort for them. But this is not what comes from his lips. Instead the attention of his listeners is directed immediately to the grandeur and greatness of God the Creator. So the elementary truth of Genesis 1:1 'In the beginning God created the heavens and the earth' is established for the benefit of this chiefly pagan audience. Accordingly Paul's next recorded words are:

God, who made the world and everything in it, since He is Lord of heaven and earth, does not dwell in temples made with hands. (Acts 17:24)

It is God as the Creator of all that can be seen and known who is proclaimed. In the gospel we are told that it is this God, our Maker, that we have to understand. Such truth is intensely humbling. This elementary fact sets the whole tone for what follows. It sets out how he is to be approached. As our Creator, he governs all the relations we are to have with him. Anything that might be said about man is determined in the light of what he tells us about himself as our Maker.

So it is no accident that in the same breath the apostle corrects the misconceptions about worship that these deceived pagan people had adopted. How could temples made with human hands offer anything meaningful to this great being who is the Maker of all? What use would he have for all these man-made efforts? The answer has to be—none at all. The whole principle is established at the outset that we have to do with a being of immense power, glory and wonder. We are having to listen to instruction about one who is far higher and superior to us. With this opening the apostle has put us firmly in our place as mere creatures before a great and awesome God.

This point is not left undeveloped by the apostle. There is a follow-up to it. We are told:

Nor is He worshipped with men's hands, as though He needed anything, since He gives to all life, and breath and all things. And He has made from one blood every nation of men to dwell on all the face of the earth, and has determined their preappointed times and the boundaries of their dwellings... (Acts 17:25-26)

This message is utterly God-centred. Not only has he revealed himself to us as Creator but we are now hearing that he is the sustainer of all things as well. We as mortals are dependent upon him from moment to moment.

c) He is a God of goodness

Taking leave of Athens for a brief moment, we find this same approach is used elsewhere when the apostles are having to deal with a Gentile and primarily pagan people. At Lystra, when the people, having witnessed a miracle, reckon that their 'gods' have come to them in human form and attempt to bring sacrifices to Paul and Barnabas, they are pointed firmly back to the Creator and Sustainer of the universe:

Men, why are you doing these things? We also are men with the same nature as you, and preach to you that you should turn from these useless things to the living God, who made the heaven, the earth, the sea, and all things that are in them. (Acts 14:15)

The Creator is also the provider of all things that are needed for man's existence:

Nevertheless He did not leave himself without witness, in that He did good, gave us rain from heaven and fruitful seasons, filling our hearts with food and gladness. (Acts 14:17)

Man has then to do with a Creator and Sustainer who does us good. He is a good God. But for all his goodness we are still ignorant of him. It is the same message at Lystra as was preached at Athens.

d) God is Sovereign

It follows on from the fact that He '...has determined their preappointed times and the boundaries of their dwellings...'(Acts 17:26) that God is the sovereign ruler over the nations. As he gives life to individuals, so he determines the times and seasons for the nations as well. God declares that all the nations exist only because he permits them.

This must have been humbling for the Greeks, who were proud of their culture and its mighty achievements. All these are put into context and thrown into relief beside God's ultimate and glorious plans. All the finery of empires and the self-exaltation of man crumbles as the apostle proclaims that nothing is achievable unless this great Sovereign and Ruler of the world had allowed it. God acts so '...*that no flesh should glory in his presence*' *(1 Corinthians 1:29)*.

e) God is holy

The God-centred nature of the gospel message is further established by showing us that this great Sovereign being is removed from us. He is unreachable by man's efforts to find and know him. He is far above man's knowing and understanding. In other words, he is holy. As for man, far from being in a position to know and understand this God, he is in a situation of weakness and in need of revelation.

Paul explains this matter to the Athenians and informs them that the reason for their being alive is:

'...so that they should seek the Lord, in the hope that they might grope for Him and find Him, although He is not far from each one of us; for in Him we live and move and have our being, as also some of your own poets have said, 'For we are also His offspring'. (Acts 17:27-28)

Poor man! He is surrounded by evidences of God's goodness and holiness but is unable to find him. Even the pagan poets are doctrinally correct without knowing it! Yet for all the fact that this Creator provides for man and gives to him every breath that he draws, despite the fact that He is the one who established the different nations and empires, none of us are any the wiser about him. He is so near—and yet so far. He is worthy of our worship, adoration and trust, but we are ignorant of him. Man is left to 'feel' after him, to grope toward him, hoping to find him but ultimately lacking light and understanding. Despite all his kindness and goodness, despite the benefits man receives from his gracious hand, man is blind and ignorant. We do not know him because he is holy and out of our reach.

f) God has to show us how to approach him

Since God is holy and separate from sinners, man is not at liberty to determine how he may approach him. This follows quite logically from all that we have already learnt about him. It is a deeply humbling and discomfiting message. God asserts the privilege and prerogative of showing to man how He is to be known and to be approached. In so doing he dismisses man's own efforts and declares them invalid and useless. Paul's proclamation to the Athenians makes this crystal clear:

Therefore, since we are the offspring of God, we ought not to think that the Divine Nature is like gold or silver or stone, something shaped by art and man's devising... (Acts 17:29)

The Lord Jesus Christ also portrays the same essential truths. It is an inescapable fact. Man is in darkness and separated from God:

For even the Son of Man did not come to be served, but to serve, and to give His life a ransom for many.(Mark 10:45)

Man is in such a plight in God's sight that 'ransom' and 'rescue' are the most appropriate terms to describe the problem. Man is far away from his Creator whom he should honour and worship. He is an outsider and in need of help to understand. Perhaps the most obvious and gripping example of this is the conversation between the Lord and Nicodemus. Here the 'teacher of Israel' (John 3:10) is shown to be ignorant and a stranger to the realities of the kingdom of God. For all the knowledge that he has, he is a foreigner to the ultimate realities about God and how he is to be approached. So he is informed in the words of the King of Glory:

Most assuredly, I say to you, unless one is born again, he cannot see the kingdom of God.(John 3:3)

So the whole matter is beyond the reach and comprehension of perhaps the wisest scholar and interpreter of the word of God in Israel at that time, the nation favoured with so many of the blessings of God (Romans 9: 4-5). Poor Nicodemus stumbles again in his understanding and has to be pointed back to the same truth, the need of divine help to see and understand:

Most assuredly, I say to you, unless one is born of water and of the Spirit, he cannot enter the kingdom of God. (John 3:5)

The evangelistic approach of the Lord himself puts man well and truly in his place. He is left to reckon with a God with whom he has no connection.

g) Man is not pleasing to God

But this God-centred message has further implications following from what we have already learnt. It is indeed the height of folly and arrogance for man to think that he is capable of knowing how God is to be pleased and worshipped. Admittedly man's ingenuity is almost limitless when it comes to inventing ways to approach God. The shrines and temples of Athens were eloquent testimony to that fact. For all man's art and complex devising, the verdict of God is not encouraging. God positively shows his extreme displeasure with such efforts.

For the wisdom of this world is foolishness with God. For it is written, "He catches the wise in their own craftiness" and again, "The Lord knows the thoughts of the wise, that they are futile". (1 Corinthians 3:19-20)

It is wrath that God expresses towards mankind. He is not at all satisfied with man's efforts and accomplishments. Far from bringing delight to his heart, man's efforts to 'feel' for God and to devise ways to approach him and worship him, incur his displeasure. This matter is left beyond a shadow of doubt in Romans 1:

For the wrath of God is revealed from heaven against all ungodliness and unrighteousness of men, who suppress the truth in unrighteousness, because what may be known of God is manifest in them, for God has shown it to them.(Romans 1: 18-19)

What is the sum of it? Man is guilty of breaking God's holy laws. *Whoever commits sin also commits lawlessness, and sin is lawlessness. (1 John 3:4)*

God's commandments about how he is to be loved and served, and how we are to behave toward him and one another have been broken and offended against. This is of the utmost gravity. For the breaking of God's laws is not an abstract principle. It means that we have sinned against God himself. It is **his** law that enshrines **his** holy character and desires. The offence is personal. We have sinned against the living God Himself.

h) Man is a sinner
God in the gospel tells us about himself. Now we are able to see what he says about man. Knowledge that has been revealed to us and proclaimed in the gospel, gives us truths about the state of mankind. Ignorant man who knows nothing of the true God, but is under his wrath, is fundamentally a sinner. He has not learnt from the things that God has done for him. He has perverted what knowledge he has into degenerate false worship, false religion and immorality (Romans 1:20-32). Whether it is the pagans of Athens or well-read and devout Nicodemus that are in view, Paul is able to assert:

For we have previously charged both Jews and Greeks that they are all under sin. (Romans 3:9)

The Jews equally with the Gentiles are guilty of rejecting God's message and incurring His wrath. They have shown themselves as sinful and ignorant as the Gentiles, despite the outward privileges the Jews enjoyed. Together with the Gentiles, '...*all have sinned and fall short of the glory of God' (Romans 3:23).*

The works of sin are visible in the evil behaviour and conduct that abound in human society. Scripture tells us '*Now the works of the flesh are evident...' (Galatians 5:19)* and lists the wicked deeds that man is capable of doing. The essence of sin lies in man himself. The misdeeds of the flesh are symptoms of the deeper problem which lies within man's heart and is to be traced to the core of his being. He is utterly sinful by nature:

...the carnal mind is enmity against God; for it is not subject to the law of God, nor indeed can be. So then, those who are in the flesh cannot please God. (Romans 8:7-8)

To say that man is a sinner is not to accuse him merely of acts of wrongdoing. Man by his very constitution and being is adrift and separated from God. His whole mind-set and heart is against God, his laws and any appreciation of his character and being. Man is not able to worship God or approach him. He is a sinner ruled over by a sinful nature and stands guilty before God. While preaching on hell is not always explicit in Acts, the implication that man is liable to judgement certainly is present. It is part of the gospel message. Using Acts 17 again, we find Paul tells the Athenians to repent:

...because He has appointed a day on which He will judge the world in righteousness by the Man he has ordained. (Acts 17:31).

Judgement is an inescapable consequence of God's holiness and man's sinfulness. It is not a comfortable truth, but God loves sinners too much to leave them in ignorance.

i) Christ the Saviour of men

We have spoken at some length about the gospel and have as yet barely mentioned Christ. How is this possible? Looking at Acts 17, we find that all the points already made about the content of the gospel are made before there is any attempt to explain what God has done to remedy the situation. The apostle Paul settles the issue of God's character and being, before presenting us with the answer to man's separation from him.

Why is this? It is because we cannot understand the work of Christ at Calvary until we are able to appreciate the holiness and majesty of God. We need to know against whom we have sinned in order meaningfully to understand what God in Christ has done to save us. It is imperative that we see that we have sinned against God himself before we can see why it required none other than his own Son to die in our place. If we do not know that we have transgressed God's law and that we are unable to remedy our situation because of our sinful nature, we will not be able to grasp why God alone could act on our behalf and why it required the death of his own Son. The cross of Christ is simply incomprehensible without having as a background the knowledge that God is holy and that sin is a personal offence against him. From this it follows that it is crucial to believe that Christ is God as well as man. The gospel involves us believing in him as the Saviour who took our place and died for us, but also that he was equipped to do this only because he was God and thus sinless. The historical facts of the life, death and resurrection of Jesus Christ now have a bearing upon the gospel as they show what God has done to save sinners. Paul explains to the Athenians that God has given assurance to the world that Christ will judge the world '...*by raising Him from the dead...'(Acts 17:31)*. It is a fact of history. If the events of the first Easter did not happen, then there is no salvation. The apostle Paul makes this evident in 1 Corinthians 15. For him the gospel involves the historical details of Christ's life and work:

For I delivered to you first of all that which I also received: that Christ died for our sins according to the Scriptures, and that He was buried, and that He rose again the third day according to the Scriptures, and that He was seen by Cephas, then by the twelve. (1 Corinthians 15:3-5)

If Christ did not do what is said of Him, if He sinned, if He did not die on the cross literally, if He did not rise from the dead bodily, then man is still in darkness and without hope in the world. So the gospel has at its heart the person and work of Christ. He is the bringer of hope, the one who offers life, the one who has done all for man's salvation. But he cannot be understood apart from the explanation that has already been given. The gospel is the message about the Son of God, who came to remedy the awful plight of man, to rescue him from the penalty of his sins and to give him the privileges of heaven.

There is of course much more that could be said. The gospel is a vast and glorious subject. We have laid some foundations that will help when we begin to evaluate the *Alpha* course. If *Alpha* fails to do justice to the gospel, we will know that it is not the answer the church needs to remedy its ills today. But before we look at that question, there are some more things that we need to know about the gospel.

More Gospel truth

We have seen what the gospel message is. But how is that message applied to us? What does it have to say to us? And what response does man have to make to it?. The gospel, we shall see, depicts a 'narrow way'. It makes no allowance for man's sensitivities, views, opinions or tastes. It is a radical message that commands our attention. It goes to the heart of man's problem, sin, and confronts him with his need of salvation.

How is the message of the gospel applied?

The message of the gospel is not left to 'hang in the air'. Because it comes from God himself it is not a piece of information of passing academic interest which is on a par with any other fact. The revelation of God's holy and just character together with his love for lost mankind is not something for us to simply note as one fact among many and then pass on our way. It has obvious and vital implications and these have to be spelled out.

a) The Gospel addresses sinners with the authority of God
The gospel, since it is not a man-made message, but from God, addresses us with God's full authority. It uncompromisingly and truthfully describes our state before God. It demonstrates that we are guilty, condemned and completely without any means of doing anything about it ourselves. Man is without wisdom to save himself. In its assessment, the gospel is infallible. It therefore requires that man admits this verdict as being true about himself. He is to assent to all that God charges him with and to accept the punishment as being just.

The Athenians are told that they have to abandon their efforts at worship. Their temples, their ideas, their creations are useless. *Truly, these times of ignorance God overlooked, but now commands all men everywhere to repent...(Acts 17:30)*

The pagans of Lystra were told to '...*turn from these useless things to the living God...' (Acts 14:15)*.

The language is that of command. It is directing us and telling us what we should do. It applies itself to listeners as those who should accept it as

God's word. This is very important. It is not a message to be idly talked about and debated. We are not free mildly and dispassionately to agree about it or reject it. Instead it comes to us as the very command of God.

Linked to this, we can say that if there is one characteristic of apostolic preaching that clamours for our attention, it is boldness. When the prayer meeting of the brethren was answered by the quaking of the room, we are told:

...they were all filled with the Holy Spirit, and they spoke the word of God with boldness. (Acts 4:31)

The church at Thessalonica was reminded by Paul that:

'...even after we had suffered before and were spitefully treated at Philippi, as you know, we were bold in our God to speak to you the gospel of God in much conflict.
(1 Thessalonians 2:2)

In the face of conflict, it would have been very tempting to 'tone down' the message a little. But this option was not available. It is the 'gospel of God'. It comes with his authority. It has to be applied to sinners so as to leave them in no doubt about its truth.

Boldness did not mean that the apostles shouted. Neither did it mean they were rude or that they were bigoted, argumentative and opinionated. Instead they unflinchingly applied the message of the gospel to their listeners and spoke as *ambassadors for Christ* (2 Corinthians 5:20). The gospel is a message that is to be urged upon people because it comes with the authority of God and is the most important information that a man can ever hear. To finish 2 Corinthians 5:20, we are to speak:

'...as though God were pleading through us; we implore you on Christ's behalf, be reconciled to God. (2 Corinthians 5:20)

Of Peter on the day of Pentecost it is said that:

'...with many other words he testified and exhorted them, saying, "Be saved from this perverse generation." (Acts 2:40)

People were to be exhorted to believe. They were to be urged and persuaded. The gospel is too important to be unapplied. It comes with the authority of God and commands man to obey.

b) The gospel leaves man with nowhere to hide
Listeners to the apostles' preaching were left in no doubt that they had disobeyed God. There was no soft soap or flattery, no trimming of the message or respect for persons. Man's guilt, folly and wickedness were uncompromisingly laid bare.

So the Jews, bearing the responsibility for putting their Saviour to death, were repeatedly reminded of their guilt. Peter's preaching on the day of Pentecost spells this out very clearly and very bluntly. Of the Lord Jesus Christ he says;

Him, being delivered by the determined purpose and foreknowledge of God, you have taken by lawless hands, have crucified, and put to death... (Acts 2:23)

Did Peter let his listeners off the hook? No. Did he spare them their blushes? No. Did he find a nice way to talk about their guilt and implication in this matter of the Lord's death? Not at all. It is set forth plainly. They are guilty and they are told so clearly. It is not surprising that after they heard this sermon '...*they were cut to the heart..*' *(Acts 2:37)*. The full horror of what they had done and where their actions had taken them dawned upon them.

Their question to the apostles, '*Men and brethren, what shall we do?*' *(Acts 2:37)* also meets with a clear and unambiguous command. '*Repent, and let every one of you be baptized...*' *(Acts 2:38)*. There was no arguing with this. Men were guilty and needed to repent. Compromise on this vital issue was not possible. It was to be received and acted upon because '...*it is in truth, the word of God...*' *(1 Thessalonians 2:13)*.

When the lame man is healed at the gate Beautiful, Peter launches forth with the following address to the crowd that has gathered, ...*you denied the Holy One and the Just, and asked for a murderer to be granted to you, and killed the Prince of life...* (*Acts 3:14-15)*.

It is a very emphatic 'you'. Nothing 'cringe-free' about this. Peter's hearers are guilty as charged and have nowhere to hide. Accordingly, the command is also given to them as it was on the day of Pentecost–'*Repent therefore and be converted...' (Acts 3:19)*. The gospel applies itself to people's hearts and tells them that they are guilty in God's sight.

c) Man needs God's help to believe

Sinners are told by the Lord himself that they must be born again to see the kingdom of God (John 3:3). It needs a work of God and the only hope of obtaining that access to God is to be shown mercy. Rightly did blind Bartimaeus call upon the Lord: "*Son of David, have mercy on me!" (Mark 10:48)*. Mercy is the pressing need of man and this is applied to sinners. They cannot save themselves. Nicodemus was taught the same thing. He needed God's help, the new birth, to enter the kingdom of God.

d) Christ alone can save

In similar fashion, it is a mark of bold gospel preaching to assert that only in Christ can salvation be found. This again follows logically from the last chapter. There we saw that God is displeased and full of wrath toward man's own solutions for his religious yearnings. Man has got the answer 'plain wrong'. Only the way that God provides is approved and consequently all others are closed off to him. The apostles told the Sanhedrin, the Jewish council, that:

> Nor is there salvation in any other, for there is no other name under heaven given among men by which we must be saved. (Acts 4:12)

Conveying truth in this way is bound to be seen as offensive. Theologian R.B. Kuiper is helpful in showing that this is intrinsic to the gospel. Having noted that the truth of salvation by grace alone is a stumbling block to people, he then writes:

> The other aspect of the Christian evangel which offends, and even infuriates, the natural man is its claim to exclusiveness. He denounces that claim as intolerant and bigoted. Yet that offensive gospel must be proclaimed without the slightest compromise, for compromise is adulteration. The truth must be spoken, the whole

truth, albeit always compassionately, patiently, and in love. (Kuiper 1994, P173)

The implications have to be spelled out. Christ alone can save. This too is a vital aspect in considering what the true gospel is.

e) The implications of rejecting the message

The way is made even more narrow by the knowledge that man cannot escape judgement if he rejects the message of life-giving grace. Paul, in his sermon at Pisidian Antioch, warns his listeners by way of conclusion:

Beware therefore, lest what has been spoken in the prophets come upon you: "Behold, you despisers, Marvel and perish! For I work a work in your days, A work which you will by no means believe, Though one were to declare it to you." (Acts 13:40-41)

Those that reject the message are warned in no uncertain terms about the consequences of so doing. They are not spared this. In the last chapter of Acts, there is again a warning issued to the disputing Jews regarding their failure to heed the message.

So when they did not agree among themselves, they departed after Paul had said one word: "The Holy Spirit spoke rightly through Isaiah the prophet, to our fathers," saying,
'Go to this people and say:
"Hearing you will hear, and shall not understand;
And seeing you will see, and not perceive;
For the hearts of this people have grown dull.
Their ears are hard of hearing,
And their eyes they have closed,
Lest they should see with their eyes and hear with their ears,
Lest they should understand with their hearts and turn,
So that I should heal them."' (Acts 28:25-27)

It is not always necessary to spell out this implication so forcefully. But it is implicit in the message that the costs of rejecting the gospel are to be made known to sinners.

There are many other implications that could be singled out as relevant. They all follow on from what we have already discovered about God's character and the 'sinfulness of sin'. We are not surprised to find that this message 'finds sinners out' and blocks off any escape routes. It is a narrow way. Christ and Christ alone can save and sinners are compelled to apply to Him for mercy. This takes us to the next section.

What response is required to the message?

All that we have already learnt about the content and implications of the gospel has been preparing us for this last and vital section. The gospel message leads to an important conclusion. It requires that sinners should **do** something. What should they do? They should repent and put their faith in Christ.

We hear this in the instruction given by Peter to the gathered crowds on the day of Pentecost (Acts 2:38). It was the command that Paul issued to the Athenians (Acts 17:30). It was the directive addressed to the people of Lystra (Acts 14:15). The same was told to the Philippian jailer (Acts 16:31). Paul's parting exhortation to the elders at Ephesus reminded them of the gospel that required '...*repentance toward God and faith toward our Lord Jesus Christ*' (Acts 20:21).

As with the content of the gospel itself, people often assume that everyone understands perfectly what repentance and faith are. But this optimism is not warranted. The Puritans spent much of their time on this very question. For them it was important to distinguish between true and false repentance, and true and false faith. We shall draw a little on some of their thinking and other modern-day thinkers who stand in that tradition. The subject can only be very briefly dealt with here, but deal with it we must in order to complete our understanding of the nature of the gospel.

a) Repentance

Repentance conveys the notion that we are to turn from our sins and all that we know to be wrong in God's sight. It is not, however, simply a change in behaviour and moral improvement. Repentance includes the idea that we have understood the content and implications of the gospel message. Modern-day theologian Paul Helm approaches the issue of repentance by describing it as follows:

Repentance is not a vague feeling of sorrow, some general mood or disposition. It is, specifically, sorrow *for sin.* It involves a change of view about ourselves, a change of mind. (Helm 1986, P49 Emphasis in the original)

Lest this be construed in a casual manner, Helm narrows it down further:

It is not a change of opinion about some relatively minor matter but a change of mind about the deepest issues in life, a person's own moral and spiritual ideals and standards, his relationship with God. This change of mind is a thorough-going reassessment. Whereas previously the individual has striven to please himself rather than to please God by keeping His law, the penitent, convinced of his own sinfulness and the fact that he both falls short of the divine standards and transgresses them, repudiates his past life. He judges it by the standard of God's law, which he now, through the Spirit's enlightening, approves of and submits to. He turns away in grief and with a deep-seated sense of unworthiness from those standards which previously governed him. (Helm 1986, P49-50)

There is a lot to think about in this carefully worded description. We are to note the radical nature of repentance. This is not a superficial self-assessment and a vague feeling of wrongdoing. It is a thorough root-and-branch examination. Man weighs himself in the scales of God's holy character and revealed purposes, and finds himself hopelessly wanting and adrift. Man sees himself as having sinned against God. His actions, attitudes and whole being are an offence to a Holy God.

This discovery is not met with indifference or casual alarm. The full implications are seen. It is a shocking discovery and the cause of sorrow. The Puritan writer and preacher of the seventeenth century, Thomas Watson, comments on the nature of true repentance:

A woman may as well expect to have a child without pangs as one can have repentance without sorrow. He that can believe without doubting, suspect his faith; and he that can repent without sorrowing, suspect his repentance. (Watson 1994, P19)

Among other things, Watson observes that there will be shame for sin and hatred of sin. It is not done by half-measures. For the Athenians, it would mean agreeing that they had acted wickedly in inventing ways of worshipping God and ignoring all the clear evidences which He had given of His true existence. It would be to agree that they were guilty and completely in the dark, 'groping' without ever finding Him. Furthermore, repentance would have taken them further and required them to accept that they were incapable of reforming themselves because of their sinful nature and to have realised that they were fit for judgement. Or for the Jews, it would mean accepting their responsibility in crucifying the Saviour whose coming was foretold in their own Scriptures but whom they wilfully and wickedly put to death.

Repentance demonstrates that we are entirely undone and with no place to hide. The man or woman, boy or girl, is 'found out'. God's holy law has been broken. Acts and deeds, whether religious or moral, are viewed in a correct light as being offensive to God and to have rightly incurred His wrath. Addressing and warning sinners another Puritan preacher, Joseph Alleine, says:

The **holiness** of God is against you. He is not only angry with you–so He may be with His children–but he has a fixed habitual displeasure against you. God's nature is infinitely contrary to sin, and so He cannot delight in a sinner out of Christ. (Alleine 1964, P86. Emphasis in original)

Something of this is known in true repentance. There is real sorrow at the offence caused to God Himself by breaking His holy laws. With it comes a deep desire to turn from these things and to obey God.

We can also see, in passing, that repentance ties up closely with another Biblical notion–conviction of sin. John's gospel informs us that the work of the Holy Spirit will involve piercing the hearts of men over their sin and moving them to sorrow for what they have done.

And when He has come, He will convict the world of sin, and of righteousness, and of judgment; of sin, because they do not believe in Me; of righteousness, because I go to My Father and you see Me no more; of judgment, because the ruler of this world is judged. (John 16:8-11)

Following Helm's helpful analysis again, we learn:

Part of God's work in conversion is to convince men that certain of the things that they do, or want to do but cannot bring themselves to do, are against the law of God, and also that they omit to do many of the things that God requires of them. The Holy Spirit not only convinces such people that they do certain things that are wrong and omit to do what is right, but He also convinces people that such corrupt behaviour springs from a corrupt source. He shows a person that his own innermost desires and intentions which give rise to his actions are not in accordance with the will of God. (Helm 1986, P25-26)

Conviction and repentance are clearly linked. Conviction brings the knowledge of man's fatal state without God. Repentance is when conviction flowers into a fruitful response. Why is it fruitful? What makes it fruitful? It is because there is side by side with it an understanding of how Christ's sacrifice is able to save them. True repentance is inseparably linked to saving faith. Helm makes the point admirably:

...true repentance arises in the context of a person's trust in the mercy of God as this is revealed in Christ. True repentance and saving faith are the inseparable twin gifts of God the Holy Spirit, the Spirit of Christ, to an individual. (Helm 1986, P67)

So we ask our next and final question, 'What is faith?'

b) Faith
Put very simply, faith is the trust that the sinner, awakened to his or her need of a Saviour, puts in the finished work of Christ. It embraces the historical facts of his person, his incarnation, his perfect life, his sinlessness, his death, his resurrection, his ascension and reign in glory, as well as his return to be the Judge of the world. Faith takes stock of the helpless condition of man by nature and then relies upon Christ for forgiveness and eternal life.

R.B. Kuiper explains it by saying of a sinner:

As to himself, he must know that he is a sinner who needs salvation, that he cannot possibly save himself, and that salvation is by the grace of the Triune God. The abandonment of himself to that grace is the essence of saving faith. (Kuiper 1994, P143)

This abandonment is tied up very closely with the understanding that Christ alone can save. It is the application of this truth in particular that leads to the abandonment of the sinner to Christ. The sinner is 'compelled' to come to Christ. He cannot save himself but he sees that Christ's death upon the cross can meet his need. True repentance and saving faith spring up together. The sinner can look nowhere else but to the mercy of Christ. He has been convinced of the evil of looking elsewhere or trying other ways to approach and please God. All else has failed–worse still, it has actively incurred God's displeasure. Only God can remedy the situation and only believing in the Saviour's work upon Calvary will suffice. Real and genuine contrition makes one tender to the command to believe in Christ.

Helm makes some good distinctions to help us understand more clearly how faith brings the benefits of Christ's death and resurrection near. It is not simply belief in some abstract piece of information nor simply a belief in the historical fact of Christ's death. Rather it is more directly and immediately an encounter with God Himself:

Faith is faith in the word of God and such faith is faith in God Himself. What the believer believes in essence is that Christ is the Saviour of sinners and that whoever comes to Him will be saved, and the believer entrusts himself to Christ...In entrusting himself to Christ he is saved, and entrusting himself to Christ means casting himself upon His mercy. It is not believing that He has been merciful, but trusting Him for mercy. (Helm 1986, P69)

In saving faith, the wonderful love of Christ is understood for the first time in its true light. Having discovered God is holy and that man is lost, it occurs to the sinner as something extraordinary that God should have done anything to save him or her, let alone send His own perfect and sinless Son. Saving faith receives the Saviour, the God of love, as offered in the gospel. It relies upon the mercy that is shown there and delights in it. The Puritan Thomas Watson puts it well when he writes:

Confession of sin endears Christ to the soul. If I say I am a sinner, how precious will Christ's blood be to me!...So when we confess the debt, and that even though we should ever lie in hell, we cannot pay it, but that God should appoint his own Son to lay down his own blood for the payment of our debt, how is free grace magnified and Jesus Christ eternally loved and admired! (Watson 1994, P35)

Faith gladly abandons itself to this Saviour of such infinite love and compassion. Christ and Christ alone can satisfy. Such trusting abandonment, as we saw when looking at repentance, necessarily means an acceptance of the Lordship of Christ and a commitment to obey him. The Lord Jesus Christ has proved himself able to save because he is God Himself and the Judge of men. As our Creator and the one to whom we owe all as creatures, not least our salvation, it follows that we must entrust everything to him. Saving faith is the resignation of the human will to God entirely. All affections and desires are now submitted to him. Our lives and substance are put at his disposal.

True repentance and saving faith always mean a decisive turning from a self-centred life. It signals the loss of independence and the acceptance in principle of all God's commands and the following of God's will. Commenting upon the example of the rich young ruler in Mark 10, Walter Chantry observes:

Practical acknowledgment of Jesus' Lordship, yielding to His rule by following, is the very fibre of saving faith...Believing is obeying. Without obedience, you shall not see life! Unless you bow to Christ's sceptre, you will not receive the benefits of Christ's sacrifice. This is just what Jesus said to the ruler. (Chantry 1989, P60)

Of course, no two conversions are the same. The experience of repentance and faith will vary. The order in which they occur will differ. What is key, however, is that there will have been an **experience**. The knowledge of God revealed in the gospel and its implications will have become real to the person. Far from being heard with studied indifference, through the working of the Holy Spirit, repentance and faith will have been imparted and **experienced**. There will be comprehension, at least in some form, of the content of the gospel. Its authority and implications will have been appreciated. There will be some capacity, even if minimal and rudimentary, to verbalise some of these things. This will not be done in theological terms, but it will be capable of being translated into such language.

In essence, if there has been true repentance and saving faith, something has **happened** to the person which is capable of being put into words, however imperfect.

Of course the theological understanding of a young convert will be imperfect. Many of the practical implications about Christ's Lordship will be only faintly grasped, and will need a lifetime to attempt to put into operation. Yet there will still be evidences that God's Spirit has been at work: *'By their fruits you will know them' (Matthew 7:20)*. The new life will come through even though the place and date of birth is not absolutely clear. Signs of life will come.

That is as far as we will take this discussion for the present. We have looked at the content of the gospel in respect of the information that it conveys. We have seen the restrictive and discomfiting implications that it entails. We have also seen that it requires us as sinners to repent and put our faith in Christ. Where these characteristics are present, we are in a position to say that the gospel has been preached or communicated. To the extent that some or many of these features are absent, we are in a position to say that the presentation is defective.

The gospel according to Alpha

The claims that are made for *Alpha* are primarily on the grounds of its runaway evangelistic success. *'It works'* and appears to raise to a new level of efficiency the winning of souls to Christ. We need then to look in more detail at what *Alpha's* evangelistic material actually teaches.

As we have seen in Chapter Two, this is dealt with in the first three weeks of the course. We are in fact quite limited in our choice of material. So what do we learn in these first three weeks? We will look at this in some detail to get a 'feel' for the evangelistic argument *Alpha* develops. Our source is *'Questions of Life'*, the basic text book of the course. This is the basic material for most of the substantive content of the video presentation of *Alpha*. There are some variations between the two. The videos contain less information than *'Questions of Life'* and omit some of the material. Essentially, however, the videos follow the book closely.

1. The Message of Week One: Christianity – Boring, Untrue and Irrelevant?

The introductory lesson deals with objections to believing in the Christian faith. Some familiar arguments against believing are put forward on the basis of Nicky Gumbel's own experience. For him the crux of the matter before he became a Christian was that Christianity seemed boring, untrue, and irrelevant. This is the starting point and the working hypothesis that Gumbel uses to address the average 'attender' on the course, 'watcher' of the video or 'reader' of *'Questions of Life'*.

The argument then explores the crises of society in the present age. These crises are illustrated using the words of secular and 'Christian' commentators. Many of the quotations are very appropriate and make the point well. With their help, we are told that modern people inhabit a world that is lost, confused and dark.

a) Living in a lost world
In this part of the course, course participants are told of man's need for a relationship with God, the absence of which will leave him with a hunger or emptiness. People try to fill this emptiness in various unsatisfactory ways. Christianity offers a better quality of life as an alternative to living in a lost world (Gumbel 1997b, P16). It will be able to help us out of our problems. The way forward will become clearer and we would not want to exchange this new-found direction for what we previously had.

b) Living in a confused world
For those living in a confused world *Alpha's* remedy is the truth of God. Christianity basically offers something to people that is true. This means that its message cannot be reduced to something that it is 'OK for you but not for me'. If its facts are true facts, they are 'true for you and true for me'. *Alpha* makes the point that Christianity is not simply about accepting something as true intellectually but is about experiencing a relationship with Christ, the truth personified (Gumbel 1997b, P18).

One effect of this experience of Christ is that our view of the world will change. Christianity will be able to make sense of the world for us. We will see things more clearly and observe the world through 'new eyes'.

c) Living in a dark world
The final section in the first session analyses the sadness of life without Christ. The reason for this is correctly located in the fall of man. (Gumbel 1997b, P18-19). The testimony of C.S.Lewis is cited as an example of someone who thought he was a good man but then made the startling discovery that the contrary was true. What is the solution to this?

We all need forgiveness and only in Christ can it be found...What Jesus did when he was crucified for us was to pay the penalty for all the things that we have done wrong...We will see that he died to remove our guilt, to set us free from addiction, fear and ultimately death. He died instead of us. (Gumbel 1997b, P19)

Christ's death is therefore offered as an answer to the problems of living in a dark world with its ills and evils. His death somehow brings us forgiveness from our evil ways. To try to understand Christ's death, Gumbel appeals to the self-sacrifice of Catholic priest, Maximilian Kolbe, who voluntarily died in the place of another prisoner in Auschwitz. It is a very powerful testimony. It is actually absent from the video of this lesson and resurfaces instead in Week Three. Nevertheless, from this the death of Christ is portrayed as being 'so much more' than even this remarkable act of love.

Jesus' death was, indeed, even more amazing because Jesus died, not just for one man, but for every single individual in the world. If you or I had been the only person in the world, Jesus Christ would have died instead of us to remove our guilt. When our guilt is removed we have a new life. (Gumbel 1997b, P20-21)

After a brief discussion of the eternal quality of the life that Christ brings, Gumbel concludes the first session by latching on to some words of liberal theologian Paul Tillich. The human condition is marked by fear about meaninglessness, death and guilt. Christ, it is claimed, '...*meets each of these fears head on*' *(Gumbel 1997b, P22)*. The video concludes in addition with an invitation to pray the 'sinner's prayer'.

The Message of Week Two: Who is Jesus?

Week Two is entitled '*Who is Jesus?*' Here *Alpha* tries to tackle head on the problems that people have in believing the Christian message and aims to dispel any doubts we may have about the historical facts of the life, death and resurrection of Jesus Christ, and in particular his claims to be God.

As a foundation for this, the reliability of the Scriptures are asserted with reference to the opinions of scholars as to the dates of the early New Testament manuscripts. This matter settled, Gumbel then feels able to use the Bible to build up the case that the Lord Jesus was not merely a man but also God.

Pursuing this, *Alpha* firstly looks at the things which the Lord said about Himself. The Lord is portrayed as the one who can give satisfaction and a relationship with God. Secular psychologists are brought in as witnesses for the defence.

There is a deep hunger within the human heart. The leading psychologists of the twentieth century have all recognised this. Freud said, 'People are hungry for love.' Jung said, 'People are hungry for security.' Adler said, 'People are hungry for significance.' Jesus said, 'I am the bread of life' (John 6:35). In other words, 'If you want your hunger satisfied, come to me.' (Gumbel 1997b, P27-28)

The historical Christ is able to provide solutions for the emotional problems of society today.

Secondly *Alpha* looks at Christ's claims to forgive sins and to be the judge of the world (Gumbel 1997b, P29-30). It examines some of His direct claims to be God, and the deity of Christ is unambiguously asserted and defended (Gumbel 1997b, P31-32). Supporting evidence for these claims is found in the fact that his teachings have had an extraordinary effect on society; that his miracles were indisputable; that his character was perfect; and that he fulfilled Old Testament prophecy (Gumbel 1997b, P32-36).

Finally the facts of the resurrection are reviewed and efforts to explain them away put firmly in their place, again with the help of C.S.Lewis. (Gumbel 1997b, P36-41) Week Two closes at this point.

The Message of Week Three: Why did Jesus die?

This the most important evangelistic section. The question it attempts to answer touches the heart of the Christian faith. We will therefore look at it in some detail:

Alpha approaches this subject by speaking about 'man's greatest need'–the problem of sin.

If we are honest, we would all have to admit that we do things which we know are wrong. Paul wrote: 'All have sinned and fall short of the glory of God.' (Romans 3:23). In other words, relative to God's standards we all fall a long way short. If we compare ourselves to armed robbers or child molesters or even our neighbours, we may think we come off quite well. But when we compare ourselves to Jesus Christ, we see how far short we fall. (Gumbel 1997b, P44)

Sin then is to be recognised by what we do and what we find in our hearts. It is more or less self-evident. None of us are as perfect as Christ. Any reasonable person would admit this. And what causes sin? *Alpha* tells us that '*...the root cause of sin is a broken relationship with God*' *(Gumbel 1997b, P44)*. How a broken relationship with God can be the 'root cause of sin' is not explained. Instead *Alpha* asks a rather curious question:

'Sometimes people say, 'If we are all in the same boat, does it really matter?' The answer is that it does matter because of the consequences of sin in our lives...'(Gumbel 1997b, P44-45)

These consequences which, for *Alpha*, constitute the heart of the problem are:

1. The pollution of sin- sin makes us unclean. One offence '*...is enough to mess up our lives.*' *(Gumbel 1997b, P45)*.

2. The power of sin–sin is addictive, its power over us is difficult to break.

3. The penalty for sin–just as we feel the need for justice in the world, so God is going to have a reckoning with us over sin.

4. The partition of sin–sin erects a barrier between us and God. The result is:

...a spiritual death which results in eternal isolation from God. This cutting off from God begins now...The things we do wrong cause this barrier. Gumbel 1997b, P46-47)

So *Alpha* focuses our attention on the consequences of sin for ourselves. We are losing out. We have our 'lives in a mess', are captive to sin, will suffer some form of punishment and will be separated from God. Sin matters because it matters to us. Christ's death is then brought alongside man's condition as an antidote:

The good news of Christianity is that God loves us and he did not leave us in the mess that we make of our own lives. He came to earth, in the person of his Son Jesus, to die instead of us (2 Corinthians 5:21; Galatians 3:13).(Gumbel 1997b, P47)

Quite ingenuously Gumbel then details Christ's achievement for us under four headings that relate to the four consequences of sin that we have just observed. In the order that these appear in *Alpha* we are told to think of Christ's achievement in four contexts:

1. **The Law Court**–we are declared 'not guilty' by God. The Judge himself pays the penalty for our sins. Christ thereby deals with the **penalty** of sin.

2. **The Market Place**–Christ pays the debts we owe. The result is that we are set free from the **power** of sin.

3. **The Temple**–following the pattern of Old Testament sacrifices at the temple, Christ made the ultimate sacrifice to cleanse us from sin. With this the **pollution** of sin is removed.

4. **The Home**–Christ's death enables us to enjoy again the relationship with God that was broken by sin. The example is that of the prodigal son who returns home. With this the **partition** of sin is solved.

Alpha now moves to conclude the section. Following an appeal and the conversion testimony of the late John Wimber, founder of the charismatic Vineyard Movement, people are then invited to pray a 'prayer of commitment.' With this being the third week, the evangelistic part of *Alpha* is finished.

This description has been brief. There are many other quotations, Scripture references and illustrations that have not been included. We now go on to see how adequate the presentation of the gospel actually is.

The missing heart of Alpha

We are now in a position to examine the gospel content of the *Alpha* course. Our considerations of the gospel in Chapters Three and Four have laid the foundations of what we should expect to find. Chapter Five has sketched the outline of the evangelistic component. What can we say as we compare them? Does *Alpha* proclaim the apostolic gospel?

There's not much gospel

It comes as something of an anticlimax to have to report at the outset that the amount of material that is recognisably evangelistic in *Alpha* is actually very small. It is just three lessons out of 15. Even allowing for the fact that Bible teaching and the 'washing of the Word' can bring life even when there is no obvious applied gospel content, it is puzzling that the proportion of the course devoted to making the gospel comprehensible to the unconverted is in reality extremely small. If we were looking for the relentless pursuit of sinners to win them to Christ or constant appeals to their consciences, we would look in vain.

So we find by the fourth week of *Alpha*, the topic has moved on to that of assurance—'*How can I be sure of my faith?*'. *Alpha* believes by then that enough has been imparted to the course participants for them to have made an adequate response. After Week Three, the attitude becomes an inclusive '*Now we are all Christians*' approach. From then onwards, the problems discussed are mostly those that would apply to Christians. Indeed Nicky Gumbel's style perceptibly changes and he now lets us in to the secrets of his own struggles and doubts when he became a Christian.

We only have to consider the title of this fourth session, '*How can I be sure of my faith?*', to realise that people risk being seriously misled. By praying the 'sinner's prayer' at the end of Week Three, it assumes that we have now picked up some 'faith' for which we need the assurance that Week Four offers. But there is nothing in Week Four to test whether true repentance and saving faith have been experienced by the course participant. There is nothing to check whether there has been a real grasp of the need for divine mercy or an understanding that Christ and he alone can save. The counsel of Week Four might be highly appropriate for new believers but is downright misleading if people are still unconverted.

It is therefore curious that a course claimed to be an 'evangelistic success' actually has very little space devoted to the gospel and to evangelistic reasoning.

It gets in a muddle here

We can take this last point further. It risks misleading people because *Alpha* is muddled in its aims.

By its own admission, *Alpha* is both for new Christians and non-Christians. It is trying to meet the needs of both. In so doing it betrays its origins. Having originally been designed as a pastoral tool to disciple new believers, it subsequently took on a life of its own and spawned an evangelistic role as well. But in reality all this manages to do is introduce an element of confusion. Who is the course really for? Is the person being spoken to as a non-Christian, a young Christian or what?

This is most disturbingly evident when it comes to the teaching on the Holy Spirit. While of course it is entirely appropriate to speak about the Trinity and to teach about the Third Person of the Godhead, the approach is confusing. For example, Lesson Nine '*What does the Holy Spirit do?*' is concluded in the following way:

God wants to fill every one of us with his Spirit. Some people are longing for this. Some are not so sure that they want it—in which case they do not really have a thirst. If you do not have a thirst for more of the Spirit's fullness why not pray for such a thirst? God takes us as we are. When we thirst and ask, God will give us 'the free gift of the water of life'. (Gumbel 1997b, P152)

The language is very inclusive. We are all being spoken to here as if we are Christians. Even if, for the moment at least, we regard in an uncritical way the standard Pentecostal/Charismatic theology of 'baptism in the Spirit', experiences such as 'speaking in tongues' are normally thought to follow, not precede conversion. To try to persuade a non-Christian to 'receive the Spirit' would be a contradiction in terms. How could they? They have not yet put their faith in Christ. Yet this is the advice that is given on the *Alpha* course. We find the following piece of indiscriminate and inclusive encouragement given during Lesson Ten, '*How can I be filled with the Spirit?*':

If you would like to be filled with the Spirit you might like to find someone who would pray for you. If you don't have anyone who would be able to pray for you, there is nothing to stop you from praying on your own. (Gumbel 1997b, P166)

So the invitation is thrown wide open. If we would like to be 'filled with the Spirit' then we can be, according to this. There is 'nothing to stop us' praying for ourselves to receive the gift. The fact that we may not actually be converted does not come into the equation. A non-Christian could easily respond to this invitation and quite likely end up 'speaking in tongues'. It is highly muddled, even using the standard terminology of Pentecostal/Charismatic theology. Only Christians who know Christ can truly thirst for the filling of the Spirit. Non-Christians need conversion, not to be filled with the Spirit.

More perceptive course leaders may be alive to this problem. Many would perhaps not make the mistake of assuming that everyone is automatically a Christian after Week Three. But they would have to work this out for themselves. The course itself gives them no guidance. Although there are various training and leadership manuals, course leaders and leaders of small groups are given no practical help in discerning whether the person is a believer or not. Neither does the course after Week Three contain anything else that would challenge unbelievers to ask whether they have truly put their faith in Christ. After Week Three the course presses ahead on the assumption that everybody is now 'on board'.

Where Alpha has nothing to say

Whatever else might be said about the course, it does use Scripture. There is unambiguous belief in the deity of Christ. It does have some apt illustrations, some of which work very well. There are contemporary figures easily recognisable as part of this culture whose own lack of light on spiritual matters is amply described.

But for all this the course is not an adequate presentation of the gospel.

Alpha fails to do justice to the message as we find it in Acts. It at times gets close to the gospel. It even deals with facts that are vital to the gospel. But it is not the gospel message. As well thought out as it is, it betrays itself at key points. Let us now look at some of its critical weaknesses.

a) Where is God?

We remember that the gospel is a message that comes from God and is about God. He is at the heart of it. Man only fits into the picture inasmuch as he relates to God. *Alpha* goes the other way about it. Its message is essentially about us.

Let us recall how Week One begins. *'Boring, untrue and irrelevant'* are the views of the Christian faith it sets out to dispel. Now of course it is important to be relevant to the needs of today's society. But somehow, *Alpha* never seems able to get away from us and our problems. This is the 'key-note' that runs throughout *Alpha's* evangelistic section. We remember the use of secular psychology and its findings on our fears, our needs and our existential questions. Christ is presented as the One who comes to meet these needs. *Alpha's* 'God' is a 'God' there essentially to rescue us out of the 'mess we have got our lives into'. Everything is related to us from our perspective. Christ dies to rescue us from the consequences of **our** sin and to save us from **our** lost, confused and dark worlds. Christ comes to remedy **our** fears. This is the bulk of the material in Week One and comes through strongly in the other two evangelistic weeks as well.

The apostolic model for preaching and teaching the gospel, as we have seen, is to begin with God. It is the God who made heaven and earth that is proclaimed (Acts 17:23-24). But no one as remotely glorious as this God impinges upon us in *Alpha*. *Alpha* does not require us to adjust ourselves radically to the knowledge of this God and his requirements. In fact in *Alpha* we learn more about ourselves and virtually nothing about God in the first three sessions. It is all about our problems, our fears, our confusion, our need for direction in life. This is quite staggering. Nicky Gumbel, having told us that his own problem was initially that he knew nothing about Christianity, then proceeds to tell us practically nothing about God. Thinking back to Acts 17 and Paul's visit to Athens, *Alpha* manages to preserve God as the 'Unknown God'. It does not proclaim him to us as Paul did. We discover next to nothing about him, his purposes, his character, and his being. At root, *Alpha* is man-centred, not God-centred.

b) No Creator, no God of glory...
This under-emphasis on God himself becomes a recurrent theme. So we find, for example, that the righteousness and holiness of God's being and character scarcely receive any attention. In fact it is not even thought worth a mention that God is the great Creator.

This point cannot be made emphatically enough. We are not speaking of optional extras but fundamental issues. If we cast our minds back to Acts 17 and Paul's preaching to the Athenians, these people were crucially ignorant of God just as we are today. They did not know how high and lofty he was. They did not know how much they owed to him as their Creator. Surrounded as they were by evidences of his goodness and kindness, they did not know how profoundly ungrateful they were to him as the great and mighty Creator. In *Alpha* God is simply introduced to us as one who can help us rather than as the self-existent and eternally glorious Maker of heaven and earth.

c) Love and nothing but love
The only thing *Alpha* does manage to convey to us about God is that He is a God of love. This is its message over and over again. It is so with the written material. It is even more so with the videos. The third session makes this emphasis plain:

God loves each one of us so much and longs to be in a relationship with us as a human father longs to be in a relationship with each of his children. It is not just that Jesus died for everyone. He died for you and for me; it is very personal.
(Gumbel 1997b, P53)

Now of course there is love in the heart of God. It is infinite love, wonderful love, perfect love. But *Alpha's* God of love is not the Biblical God of love.

The God of the Bible is a God of holiness whose love is all the more remarkable in that it is bestowed upon wicked sinners. It is expressed by one who is holy and glorious. That is what makes the love of Christ comprehensible and meaningful. *Alpha* has not adequately told us about the character of this God. So his love ends up being mere emotion and sentiment. Unless we are conscious of how sinful we are and what a great act of mercy it was for God to give his Son for us, we will never understand the love of God. Until we see ourselves as guilty sinners, we have no vantage point to grasp his love or to understand why Christ died. It is like trying to describe what it is to be thirsty to someone who has never had the experience. There is no point of connection.

d) No sin...
In *Alpha* Christ comes to rescue us from the consequences of our sin. He loves us and has come to save us from our hapless human condition. In the Bible, Christ comes not only to rescue us from the **consequences** of sin but supremely to meet the **requirements** of God's holy law. It is a vital distinction.

The root of sin is that it is an offence against the holy law of God. It is to underplay the gravity of this seriously when *Alpha* tells us that the '*...root cause of sin is a broken relationship with God...*' *(Gumbel 1997b, P44)*. This does not go anything like far enough. Sin is the breaking of God's law and therefore an offence against the person of God himself. This is what is fundamental to the broken relationship with God and is of the utmost importance. *Alpha* simply has no grasp of the holiness of God and of his wrath against sin. It has no concept of man having offended God.

This explains why *Alpha* curiously answers the question 'why worry about sin' by listing four **consequences** of sin. The consequences are true enough. But it is all man-centred. They are the consequences **for us**. Surely the fact that we have offended against God is sufficient reason in itself for us to worry about sin? But *Alpha* has not told us about the holiness of God and so has no point of reference to introduce concepts such as this. Instead it has to resort to its 'four consequences' to answer its question 'why worry about sin'. *Alpha's* analysis simply does not go anything like far enough. Its 'Christ' comes forth to deal with too small a problem.

This problem surfaces again and again. It is no surprise to find that the 'Christ' of *Alpha* was crucified '*...to pay the penalty for all the things that* *we have done wrong.' (Gumbel 1997b, P19 My emphasis)*. It is true indeed that sin is evident in the things *'we have done wrong'*. But there is so much more to sin than simply this. It is far worse than what we know about ourselves or experience in our lives. It is worse even than failing to live as perfectly as the Lord Jesus. We are incurably sinful and are *'...by nature children of wrath...' (Ephesians 2:3)*. It is not just what we do–it is what we are in God's sight that is the problem.

Hand-in-glove with this failure, is the lacklustre handling of the 'temple' scene in the section looking at 'consequences of sin'. There we are told that the sacrificial system shows *'...the seriousness of sin and the need for cleansing from it' (Gumbel 1997b, P52)* but we are not told why it is serious. The question is simply begged. Why is sin so serious that it requires death? Why did it ultimately require the death of God's own Son? Instead we are told that it removes the *'...pollution of sin.' (Gumbel 1997b, P52)*. Is that all? Has this adequately explained to us the function of the sacrificial system? Has this proved why sin is serious and needs such a drastic remedy? *Alpha* misses the point entirely. Death is required because God's law states *'The soul who sins shall die' (Ezekiel 18:4)*. There is far more to it than *Alpha* allows.

e) No wrath, no judgement...
Neither will it come as something unexpected to find that the 'God' of *Alpha* is not a God of wrath. The concept is not even mentioned. Neither is anger, nor is there any equivalent illustration to convey this notion to us. The Athenians to whom Paul preached were left in no misapprehension that their efforts at worship did not meet with the approval of the King of Glory. Or as we find in the words of John the Baptist:

He who believes in the Son has everlasting life; and he who does not believe the Son shall not see life, but the wrath of God abides on him. (John 3:36)

Alpha does not make us aware of the grave situation we are in with the wrath of God abiding on us.

The nearest *Alpha* can get to the concept of holy wrath is when discussing the 'law-court scene', one of the antidotes to the consequences of our sin. We are guilty and Christ pays the price for us. He is therefore '*...both our Judge and our Saviour.*' (Gumbel 1997b, P50). But it is by no means clear what this implies. In fact, it is not a central argument in *Alpha*, but surfaces in a roundabout fashion buried among the results that Christ's death secures for us. It is more an after-thought than something that is built into the very fabric of the course. We would need to know far more about the nature of God's judgement and the basis of his judgement than this before we could be in any position to appreciate the consequences of what Christ has done for us.

As a final example of how *Alpha* misses the gravity of sin, the subject of judgement itself is only alluded to *sotto voce*. *Alpha* tiptoes through it so quietly, we may easily be forgiven for missing it. We are told that '*...we will all be subject to the judgement of God*' (Gumbel 1997b, P46) but not informed how awesome this will be. The video for Week Two tells us that there will be a separation of sheep and goats but does not properly develop this. Scripture tells us '*It is a fearful thing to fall into the hands of the living God*' (Hebrews 10:31). Scripture tells us of the terrors that await the impenitent there who '*...shall be punished with everlasting destruction from the presence of the Lord and from the glory of his power...*' (2 Thessalonians 1:9). *Alpha* is fairly silent on this point. The torments of hell and judgement are watered down to the expression '*...eternal isolation from God*' (Gumbel 1997b, P46) and that is it—no more to be said. From top to bottom, having failed to tell us what God is like, *Alpha* cannot tell us what sin is and why it is subject to the wrath of God.

f) Missing the point of Christ's work on the Cross

What we are left with in *Alpha* is a 'God' who feels sorry for us. Its central message is that he loves us all intensely and longs for us to believe in him. *Alpha* thinks that our problem is that we have not realised how much he loves us and that if we did, we would be more likely to respond to him. Its case rests upon the fact that God sent his Son to die for us. This is the demonstration of love that forms the central basis of its appeal. It is then for us to see the Cross in personal terms (Gumbel 1997b, P53), and enter into the benefits—freeing us from the consequences of sin and bringing us into a relationship with a loving God.

It is not too difficult to see that there is much truth in all of this. People are empty. They do need God. Life without him is meaningless. The consequences of sin are screaming at us to be recognised as such. God does care for the plight of man. Yet *Alpha* is unable to get to grips with the meaning of why Christ **had** to die. In *Alpha* the danger is that the Cross becomes reduced to some 'visual aid' which conclusively proves that God is self-sacrificial and loving. Christ's work on the Cross is demoted to being a rescue act to save us from our problems rather than fulfilling the righteous demands of the holy law and appeasing the wrath of God.

The clue that *Alpha* is all at sea on the issue of the atonement is to be found in the illustration that it uses in Week Three to explain the death of Christ. For a suitable parallel, Gumbel takes us to the River Kwai in the Second World War and the remarkable bravery of a British soldier. This man was part of a working party building the Burma Railway for the Japanese. One day a guard noticed that a shovel was missing. The guard:

...began to rant and rave, working himself up into a paranoid fury and ordered whoever was guilty to step forward. No one moved. 'All die! All die!' he shrieked, cocking and aiming his rifle at the prisoners. (Gumbel 1997b, P47)

At this point the brave soldier volunteers that it was he who took the shovel and is promptly clubbed to death although in point of fact no shovels were missing. The prisoner was simply doing this to protect the others. It was, in other words, an action of immense courage. Gumbel tells us *'In the same way Jesus came as our substitute'* (Gumbel 1997b, P48). But does this illustration help us understand why Christ had to die? The answer is that it does not.

Consider it for a moment. The 'justice' which the brave soldier endured was not the justice of a holy and good God. It was the arbitrary and cruel wickedness of a ruthless tyrant. The Japanese guard worked himself into a 'paranoid fury' and shrieked over a relatively minor matter. Is this really a picture of the justice of God and of His holy wrath? Is the wrath of God the Father comparable to the rage of a wicked man reacting over a minor offence? *Alpha* does not explicitly say this of course but the illustration gets us nowhere in our search to understand why Christ died. It simply tells us that the soldier was very courageous and very self-sacrificial. This does not get us to the heart of the matter. Neither is it helpful to compare the action of a man who dies in point of fact for a non-existent offence with the death of Christ. The Lord Jesus Christ had to die for real offences–our offences against a holy God. The illustration gets us nowhere. It may convey something of the pain and agony which the Saviour experienced but it does not tell us why He **had** to die. Without a clear explanation of transgression against God's holy laws, there is no coherent explanation that can be given.

The video at this point substitutes the occasion of Maximilian Kolbe's self-sacrifice to make the point. But this too has the same basic flaw. In this situation, Kolbe volunteers to take the place of another man when the concentration camp officers select prisoners to die as a reprisal for an escape. There is no point of comparison, however, between the injustices and wickedness of the Nazi-run concentration camp and the holy laws of God. The illustration fails to illustrate in exactly the same way as the event from the River Kwai.

Alpha tries a few more times to explain the matter to us but fails. We are told that God had to punish Christ, His Son, and in so doing '*He made it possible for us to be restored to a relationship with him.*' *(Gumbel 1997b, P52).* But the whole thing is mystical. It had to happen but we do not know why. It is a mysterious transaction that is not clearly explained. In Week One we are told that he died to '*...remove our guilt. When our guilt is removed we have a new life.*' *(Gumbel 1997b, P21)* But we are never told why his death was necessary to remove our guilt. A sufficiently compelling reason is never found because there is never any real grasp of the holiness of God or the wrath of God. All we are left with is love without a context seen in the self-sacrifice of Christ who died in order to make our lives better. Is this really the end of the story?

Evangelism or Apologetics?

Finally, we may have observed that little mention has been made of the material of Week Two, '*Who is Jesus?*'. The reason is simple. Its material is apologetic rather than evangelistic. We need to be clear about the difference. Apologetics is the branch of Christian thought that offers historical and other supporting evidence to back up what the Bible teaches.

It draws upon archaeology, history, philosophy and logic as well as other disciplines to provide additional testimony for the truth of the Bible. Yet for all its undoubted value and usefulness, it is not evangelism. The gospel is evangelism.

How then shall they call on him in whom they have not believed? And how shall they believe in him of whom they have not heard? And how shall they hear without a preacher? (Romans 10:14)

It is God's word preached that is God's means for saving sinners. So Paul is able to say with emphasis:

For I am not ashamed of the gospel of Christ, for it is the power of God to salvation to everyone who believes, for the Jew first and also for the Greek. (Romans 1:16)

Apologetics may clear up misunderstandings. Apologetics can help remove intellectual misunderstandings or difficulties. But it is the gospel that converts. *Alpha's* defence of the deity of Christ is reasonably good. It makes the case quite well and succinctly. But by itself, it is not the gospel. Again it is important to prove that the resurrection happened. If there was no resurrection, then there is no salvation as the apostle Paul makes crystal clear (1 Corinthians 15:17). *Alpha* leaves us in no doubt that the actual event took place but does not adequately explain the significance of it. How it forcibly proves the awesome nature of Christ's claims is left for us to work out. Indeed the fact that the resurrected Lord ascended into heaven and is seated at the right hand of God is not even thought worth a mention. Neither is there any allusion to the future event when the risen Lord will return to be our Judge. It is apologetic material left hanging in the air without the real evangelistic implications being drawn out.

This is quite revealing. *Alpha* believes that the problem of conversion is basically due to want of true information about Christ. Remove the doubts and the task is practically done. So one third of the 'evangelistic' component is basically apologetic rather than the gospel *per se*. When we further recall that the first session essentially looks at modern man's problems in believing in God, we can appreciate that much of the supposedly evangelistic part of the course has drifted by without any real gospel content. It is all left to the Third Week and, as we have just seen, this is too flawed to be looked upon as reliable.

Let us sum up where we have arrived. We have seen that *Alpha* is silent on some key issues which were very much to the fore in apostolic preaching. There is a missing heart to *Alpha*–and that missing heart is God himself. Subjects such as God as Creator, the majesty and glory of his being, his holiness, his wrath against sin, and the judgement that is to come are either completely absent or else hugely understated. Sin is underplayed in its gravity and the whole approach is man-centred. When *Alpha* does speak, it begins at the wrong place–ourselves. It then misses a golden opportunity to use evangelistic arguments by reducing much of the subject matter to apologetics. Finally it is unable to give us a coherent answer as to why Christ had to die. God, it seems, has made a great gesture of love to rescue us from the consequences of our own selfish lives so as to satisfy our hunger and fulfil us.

Comparing this with material from which the preaching of the apostles was composed, we can see that we have been woefully short-changed in *Alpha*. It has taught us poor theology and failed to proclaim the God of the Bible. We have not been made sufficiently aware of the great gulf that exists between him and us. Alas, as we will see, the rest of the course makes us none the wiser about this either.

Alpha: a toothless gospel

We have seen how the evangelistic content of the *Alpha* course fails to do justice to what we find in the New Testament. There is not the clarity that there needs to be about the character of God, the 'sinfulness of sin' or the meaning of Christ's death. What can we go on to say about the approach that the apostles took in their preaching? How do their methods compare with *Alpha*? Does *Alpha* make us sufficiently aware of our responsibility? Does it properly apply its arguments to our consciences? Does it command us in the way of apostolic preaching to enter by the narrow way of repentance and faith?

Love's appeal

The nearest thing we really have to an appeal or invitation given to sinners is when *Alpha* tells us in Lesson Three, the key evangelistic part of the course:

God loves each one of us so much and longs to be in a relationship with us as a human father longs to be in a relationship with each of his children. It is not just that Jesus died for everyone. He died for you and for me; it is very personal...Once we see the cross in these personal terms, our lives will be transformed. (Gumbel 1997b, P53)

Yet again, it is all about love. This is the heart of the appeal that is made. God is 'longing' for a relationship with us and is waiting for us to wake up to this. In the language that *Alpha* uses, we are already His children. It sounds very intimate and close. We are not made remotely aware that we are sinners far away from God and far removed from His love. We are not told that we need mercy if we are ever going to enter the kingdom of God. In *Alpha*, in a sense, we are 'already there'. We just need to wake up to the fact and 'make it personal'.

Now it may come as a surprise to know that nothing like this sort of appeal ever enters the language of the apostles. It is not the love of God that they confront us with. What confronts us is mercy, not sentimental love. Until we see how far we are from God and how mercy is our great need, God's love cannot be grasped. Once we see how deserving of wrath and eternal punishment we are, we do not need to be told about the love of God. We **know** it. It explains itself. When we realise that God is willing to save wretched sinners from their sins through the cross, we **know** God's love. Apostolic preaching had no need to force us to accept a God of love. It presented a God who is holy yet willing to save sinners. There is the love. There is no place for a sentimental and emotional God who merely 'longs' for a relationship with us.

Similarly there are difficulties with saying that 'Jesus died for everyone'. *Alpha* assures course participants that He 'died for you and for me'. But the apostles never proclaim to their listeners a God who is so available and accessible to us. He will save us if we call upon His name, it is true. They never assure us, however, that he died for everyone or that he died 'for you and for me'. The apostle Paul, quoting the Lord's words to Moses in Exodus 33:19, tells us:

I will have mercy on whomever I will have mercy, and I will have compassion on whomever I will have compassion. (Romans 9:15)

The Lord appears to have a greater say in the matter of salvation and conversion than *Alpha* leads us to suppose. When Peter discerns that all is not well in the attitude of Simon the sorcerer at Samaria, he instructs him:

Repent therefore of this your wickedness, and pray God if perhaps the thought of your heart may be forgiven you. (Acts 8:22)

It is a somewhat less accessible God that is offered to Simon than the 'God' whom *Alpha* 'confronts' us with. Peter sets before Simon a God who is merciful but whose mercy has to be sought and found. We are not allowed to presume that the love is there for us but are instructed to humbly seek. One fears that if Simon had been doing the *Alpha* course, he would have been handled rather differently.

In other words, *Alpha*'s appeal is premature. It is assuring us of something beforehand that is only truly known after we are converted. We will know that God loves us and has died for us if we find His mercy. The sort of appeal that *Alpha* makes, in common with a host of other evangelistic approaches, is misleading and faulty. *Alpha's* gospel is not the one the apostles preached. It is a toothless and sentimental gospel that fails to ground the love of God in His justice.

Getting us to the point

The key third lesson, '*Why did Jesus die?*', is concluded with a testimony of the late John Wimber of how he was converted. After this participants are led into 'the sinner's prayer'. This testimony bears further examination as we are presumably meant to regard it as a model of what we are like as sinners, and an indication of what we need to know about God. Wimber states:

I thought I was a good guy. I knew I messed up here and there but I didn't realise how serious my condition was. (Wimber in Gumbel 1997b, P53)

It sounds quite good so far. There is recognition that sin is serious. It goes on to say more, however. When his wife Carol prayed at a small-group meeting that she was sorry for her sin, Wimber was sent into something of a flat spin. If she thought that she needed to admit she was a sinner, Wimber knew that the logic of this meant that he had to admit he was a sinner too. He tells us:

In a flash the cross made personal sense to me. Suddenly I knew something that I had never known before; I had hurt God's feelings. He loved me and in his love for me he sent Jesus. But I had turned away from that love; I had shunned it all of my life. I was a sinner desperately in need of the cross. (Wimber in Gumbel 1997b, P54)

Now it is not the place here to say too much about Wimber himself and whether or not he was a true believer. But there are some things which are present in this 'model conversion' which are used in '*Questions of Life*' and the video presentation that cannot be glossed over.

Perhaps the most revealing part is the phrase that he realised he had 'hurt God's feelings'. What does this mean? Did he realise that by nature he was a sinner? Did he understand that he stood deserving God's wrath and judgement? Was he aware of what peril he stood in and what God 'felt' about his unbelief and sin? It is not clear from what he has written that he did. Instead the Cross made 'personal sense' to him 'in a flash', but what came to him was less a sense of having sinned against a holy God than a feeling of 'hurting God's feelings' by having spurned His love. We are almost left feeling sorry for God! By this reading, God is actually left 'feeling hurt' that, having done so much for us in sending his Son to die, we have resolutely ignored him. As we saw in the last chapter, the Cross becomes little more then a symbol and demonstration of love, rather than the place where atonement was made for our sins. In *Alpha,* our problem essentially is that we are too dumb to recognise a good offer when it is staring us in the face. It would appear from this that *Alpha's* appeal to us is little more than that we should believe in his love. Nothing faintly like it is found in the preaching of the apostles.

Name them and shame them

If we are not confronted with the narrow way of the true and living God, it is also true that we are not confronted with the 'sinfulness of sin'. Hearers in the times of the apostles had their sins advertised very clearly. The worshippers of Lystra were informed that the sacrifices were '...*useless things...*' from which they needed to turn (Acts 14:15). The Jewish Sanhedrin were informed by Stephen that they were '...*stiff-necked and uncircumcised in heart and ears...*' *(Acts 7:51).* Nobody's blushes were spared in the preaching of the apostles and early church prophets. The preaching was very bold.

Alpha seems unwilling to follow suit. There is no extended treatment on pride or unbelief. There is no speaking out against the arrogance of man. There is no listing of sins. There is no full description of man's hopelessly sinful ways and of his irretrievably sinful nature. His wilful disobedience and rebellion against God is not placarded. *Alpha's* participants are spared this.

Instead of appearing sinful, man comes across as being rather sad. The portrait of ourselves that we are presented with is one of pathos rather than obstinate sinfulness. We are creatures in a lost, dark and confused world, making a mess of our lives, and tragically ignorant that God really does love us. Our sins are taken as evidence merely that life is not what it could or should be. We are missing out. This is *Alpha's* message to us. There is no bite, there is no confrontation of ourselves as sinners. We feel sorry for ourselves rather than ashamed of ourselves.

You can't be serious!

What we have already seen will prepare us for the next point. There is no urgency or real sense of the seriousness of our situation and of our responsibility before God. There is never any serious challenge to repent of our sins, to take stock of our lives or wake up to the danger that we are in. The course, even when supposedly at its most evangelistic, does not bristle with urgency or convey the enormity of our crime. It does not present to us the authoritative demands of God. It is not such a narrow way after all.

Throughout the course, as we saw in the last chapter, *Alpha* conceals from us the severity of God's judgement and why we need to flee to Christ for mercy. Eternal punishment and judgement are not *Alpha's* strong points. Week Four *'How can I be sure of my faith?'* quotes John 3:16 including the part that *'...whoever believes in him shall not perish...' (Gumbel 1997b, P65)* but it does not define 'perish'. This crops up again in Week Three: *'Why did Jesus die?'*

One day we will all be subject to the judgement of God. St Paul tell us that 'the wages of sin is death' (Romans 6:23)...The death Paul speaks of is not only physical. It is a spiritual death which results in eternal isolation from God. This cutting off from God begins now. (Gumbel 1997b, P46)

What is spiritual death? It is being 'cut off' from God. What is being 'cut off' from God? It is being 'eternally isolated' from God. What does being 'eternally isolated' mean? We are not told. It again sounds more sad than serious. Does it mean everlasting and conscious punishment? It does not say. Does it mean that the souls of the unconverted just go to 'sleep'? Again we are not told. In the light of the fact that the Roman Catholic church is able to embrace *Alpha* and find nothing incompatible with its own teaching, we can see that this wording does not rule out purgatory either. It is vague and undeveloped.

In passing, it is ironic to note that one of the few places where a sense of greater urgency surfaces is at the 'Holy Spirit Weekend Away' (Gumbel 1997b, P163-167). Nicky Gumbel is far more efficient at demolishing arguments against 'speaking in tongues' than at smoking out sinners from their refuges of unbelief and sinful pride. We will see this more clearly in the next chapter.

Praying the prayer

Even though there has not been an adequate presentation of the holy demands of God, of his authoritative call to us to repent and believe, *Alpha* still invites people to pray the 'sinner's prayer'. It is promised that praying this prayer will begin the Christian life for people (Gumbel 1997b, P54). The prayer proceeds as follows:

Heavenly Father, I am sorry for the things I have done wrong in my life. (Take a few moments to ask his forgiveness for anything particular that is on your own conscience.) Please forgive me. I now turn from everything which I know is wrong.

Thank you that you sent your Son, Jesus, to die on the cross for me so that I could be forgiven and set free. From now on I will follow and obey him as my Lord. Thank you that you now offer me this gift of forgiveness and your Spirit. I now receive that gift. Please come into my life by your Holy Spirit to be with me for ever. Through Jesus Christ, our Lord. Amen. (Gumbel 1997b, P 54-55)

It is interesting to note again the stress upon sin as being the '...*things I have done wrong in my life*'. The failure to confront us with our true nature and standing before God carries through into the language of the prayer. More to the point, we should not be too reassured by the presence of such words as 'sorry' or the expressions of willingness to 'turn' from what we know to be wrong. Repentance is more than the 'praying of a prayer', even a prayer with some of the right words in it. Unless there is conviction that accompanies these words and expressions, they achieve nothing despite the promise that is given by *Alpha* before the participant actually prays them. The request for forgiveness and the thanks for the gift of life are again all very well if God is really at work in the person's life, but if he is not, then they amount to nothing.

Did the apostles give 'model prayers' for people to pray? There is no evidence that they did, despite the widespread use of this practice among evangelical churches today. What is almost taken for granted today in the conduct of evangelism is absent from the New Testament. Why is this? It is because the preaching of the word of God generated the necessary feelings and convictions rather than the mechanical 'praying of a prayer'. When Peter's hearers were confronted with their guilt on the day of Pentecost, we read:

Now when they heard this, they were cut to the heart, and said to Peter and the rest of the apostles, "Men and brethren, what shall we do?" Then Peter said to them, "Repent and let every one of you be baptized in the name of Jesus Christ for the remission of sins; and you shall receive the gift of the Holy Spirit." (Acts 2:37-38)

When they were told to repent they knew what this meant because they were already '...*cut to the heart...*' because the Spirit of God was working in them. Peter could assure his listeners that they would be forgiven and receive the gift of the Holy Spirit if they truly turned to the Lord. They did not have to use a form of words. Whereas, with *Alpha,* assurance is given us because we have prayed a prayer. This is false assurance.

In fact this belies the rather mechanical understanding of conversion that is at the heart of *Alpha.* Nowhere are leaders taught how to look for the evidences that a person is truly under conviction of sin or that there is a real work of grace going on in their lives. The participant has already been promised that 'praying the prayer' will bring them into the benefits of Christ's death.

It is revealing to see the results of praying this sort of prayer in the life of one man who went to see Nicky Gumbel. The man explains:

So we went to the crypt, where I prayed a prayer of Christian commitment. He said it was like a bench mark, and that I'd probably prayed it already but hadn't formalised it. I asked Jesus to forgive me and to come in and take over my life. I didn't feel anything. It was no big deal and I went back to work. (In Elsdon-Dew (ed) 1995, P52)

Conversion 'no big deal'? Becoming a Christian a matter of 'formalising' something we probably already believed anyway? There are obviously no great expectations in *Alpha* about conversion. It happens without us knowing too much about it. It is in fact interesting to see that this part of the course is not often referred to by people who do *Alpha*. 'Praying the prayer' does not lead to great experiences of God's love and mercy. It appears to be a non-event. Take the example of another man who attended the third session of the *Alpha* course. He tells us:

I decided that I would only find out if it was true if I tried praying Nicky's prayer in his Why Jesus? booklet and asking Jesus to come into my life. So I did pray that prayer. I was sitting at home playing my favourite Van Morrison record when I just got my copy of Why Jesus? out and I prayed the prayer at the back, turning away from everything that is wrong, repenting of it and asking God to forgive me and come into my life. It had absolutely no impact upon me whatsoever. So I sort of thought, 'Well great'...Then I went on the Alpha weekend. And then something happened. (In Elsdon-Dew (ed) 1995, P60)

So much then for 'praying the prayer'. So much then for conversion to Christ—with or without the accompaniment of Van Morrison. The conversion it looks to produce is a non-event and it awaits the 'Holy Spirit Weekend Away' for an experiential supplement.

More coffee?

To conclude this section, we note that the overall concept and approach of *Alpha* is virtually built around the premise that nobody should be too offended. The approach is not direct. It is not bold and does not present people with a God who commands them to obey him. It deliberately does not strike fear in the hearts of sinners with warning of what awaits them if they fail to believe the gospel. The narrow way of repentance and true faith is not explained.

Yet this 'softly-softly' method is hailed as one of *Alpha's* virtues. With good food, friendly conversations and the 'small-group feel,' it is meant to be a light and not too serious approach to the Christian faith. In the words of the sponsors of *Alpha*:

We believe it is possible to learn about the Christian faith and have a lot of fun at the same time. Laughter and fun are a key part of the course, breaking down barriers and enabling everyone to relax together. (Alpha News February 1997, P12)

It is suggested that on a typical evening, with supper concluded, the meeting begins at 7.40pm with:

A welcome from the leader (perhaps even a joke!) and any notices are given out. This is followed by a short time of worship. (Alpha News February 1997, P25)

The videos in fact are jam-packed with jokes and funny anecdotes. Much of the substance of *'Questions of Life'* is sacrificed to make room for more jokes and stories on the videos. Even on serious topics, humour still intrudes. It is a clear message about the environment which is to be produced and maintained. On the video we are frequently shown pictures of the audience where the atmosphere seems more akin to an after-dinner speech. Into such an environment it is difficult to inject a greater note of seriousness or urgency. It almost becomes bad taste and 'ruining a good evening out' to bring too 'heavy' a message.

The 'Weekend Away' conveys the same things. Even the crowning climax of the course, the Saturday Night session on *'How can I be filled with the Spirit?'*, using the suggestions of the course organisers, is then followed at 7.30pm with supper and at 9pm with 'entertainments and revues'. (*Alpha News*, February 1997, P25). We may smile at the thought of a small struggling church with its *Alpha* 'Weekend' in a draughty church hall mounting anything as elaborate as a revue. But what it communicates to us is that this is to be light and easy. Even the pinnacle of the course, the 'experience of the Holy Spirit' is to be followed by an evening of fun.

The final lesson of the course is described as a *'supper party' (Alpha News, February 1997, P12)* akin to an end-of-term college meal. Most of the publicity shots that are used to promote the course show groups of happy and relaxed people enjoying what looks like a good evening out. Smiles and conviviality abound. Food and fun seem to be the order of the day. Now of course nobody is saying that meals and friendships are out of place and wrong. But the atmosphere which *Alpha* is deliberately generating is bound to detract from the seriousness of the message. The medium becomes the message. Attention is focussed away from the implications of the gospel for us as sinners. Instead we are made to feel that the Christian message belongs to this atmosphere of warm friendliness.

We have already seen that *Alpha* does not have much of a message with which to begin. What little it has is dissipated by misrepresenting the character of God's love, and the nature of His forgiveness. It does this by by toning down the significance of sin and the need for full repentance. It fails to emphasise the need to appeal to our consciences, and to recognise our guilt, and the responsibility that we have before God. Worse still, it even seems to think that this is a good thing! It is light years away from the method of the apostles. We go on now to see if the 'Weekend Away' supplies what is missing and rescues the day. For it is evident that the evangelistic part of the course does not do much converting. Does the 'Weekend Away' do any better?

Getting away from it all

Experience and the 'weekend away' in the Alpha course

Many of the testimonies of people who have completed the *Alpha* course hinge upon the 'Holy Spirit Weekend Away'. In its own publicity, the *Alpha* course states:

The Week-end is a crucial element of the course when the Holy Spirit is introduced. Sometimes the teaching can be incorporated into a single day, but the week-end is a good chance to cement friendships and take a break away. August 1995, P10-11)

Ideally lasting from Friday night to Sunday afternoon, it takes in the three sections on the Holy Spirit as well as a further talk on *'How can I make the most of the rest of my life?'*.

What happens at this 'Weekend Away'? What are people taught? And how does it relate to true repentance and saving faith?

The spirit of *Alpha*

Without doubt it is the session *'How can I be filled with the Spirit?* that is the vital talk at the 'Weekend Away' and perhaps in the whole course. It is at the end of this session that 'everything happens'.

As such, this session contains few surprises. All in all, it is a fairly standard apologetic for charismatic theology and practice. This holds to the view that while we have the Holy Spirit as Christians, we are not as effective as Christians until we are filled with the Spirit. As soon as someone receives the Spirit there is a marked change in the person that distinguishes them from those who have not had this experience.

To ground this, *Alpha* whisks us on a guided tour that takes in some of the key events of the Acts of the Apostles. It quickly becomes clear, however, that people are being prepared to accept phenomena and bodily manifestations as being evidences that the Holy Spirit is at work and that they are being filled with Him. Taking as its supposed model the phenomena recorded in Acts 2, the Day of Pentecost, course participants are told:

Sometimes, when people are filled, they shake like a leaf in the wind. Others find themselves breathing deeply as if almost physically breathing in the Spirit. (Gumbel 1997b, P156)

The tongues of fire of Acts 2 similarly find their counterpart according to *Alpha* in an experience:

Physical heat sometimes accompanies the filling of the Spirit and people experience it in their hands or some other part of their bodies. One person described a feeling of 'glowing all over.' Another said she experienced 'liquid heat'. Still another described 'burning in my arms when I was not hot.' (Gumbel 1997b, P156)

Others are told that they will experience the 'overwhelming love of God' and might express this in emotional ways. One way or another, the scene is being set for people to experience emotions and phenomena. People are virtually warned not to be afraid to vent their feelings or express themselves in extravagant ways. Tongues-speaking is also approved of as an outlet for us to express emotion.

Alpha then moves on to the 'appeal' and attempts to persuade people on the course to accept the gift that is offered. Gumbel describes his own initial reticence about tongues but then explains how he asked some friends to pray for him. He was told that he had to '*co-operate with the Spirit of God*' (*Gumbel 1997b, P164*). When he co-operated and opened his mouth, he began to speak in tongues. The message then is clear. Participants on the course have to do something if they want to receive this gift or any other manifestation of the Holy Spirit. They have to co-operate. To assist in this, a list of potential obstructions is given to ensure that barriers to co-operation are taken down. Among those listed are doubt, fear and inadequacy (Gumbel 1997b, P165-167). Having broached these, the course then lays down some guidelines for overcoming them. We find for example among the steps which are given, that we should:

3. Ask God to fill you with his Spirit and to give you the gift of tongues. Go on seeking him until you find. Go on knocking until the door opens. Seek God with all your heart.

4. Open your mouth and start to praise God in any language but English or any other language known to you..

5. Believe that what you receive is from God. Don't let anyone tell you that you made it up. (It is most unlikely that you have.) (Gumbel 1997b, P167).

It is a case of 'hard-sell'. People are boxed into a corner so that unless they co-operate they are 'missing' out on what the Holy Spirit wants to do. There is virtually no way out. *Alpha* assures us that 'all must have prizes' by guaranteeing that anything we say in our attempted tongues-speaking must be from God and if anyone says anything to the contrary, they are simply wrong. It is an open and shut case. So having followed the instructions, what actually happens?

What the people say

Judged by its own standards, the 'Weekend-Away' turns out to be a huge success. From the reports that are given by people who attend the *Alpha* course, it is usually this part of the course that is the most memorable. The instructions we have looked at 'work'. Plenty of things do happen.

Undoubtedly, by far and away the most important parts of the 'Holy Spirit' experience are feelings and phenomena. Here are just a few examples of the many which could have been selected:

On the weekend away I was blessed to receive the Holy Spirit. What an experience–total peace, floods of tears and a feeling that I was a special person, loved by Jesus totally. (Alpha News March 1996, P26)

I didn't want to come to the weekend and I did. But I would call myself a Christian now. I would say that I felt the Holy Spirit. I was feeling I was loved. It was really a tremendous overwhelming feeling of love. (Alpha News December 1993, P7)

But Nicky talked about the gifts and tongues, and at the end of his talk, he asked the Holy Spirit to come. I was just totally overcome. I couldn't control what was happening to me. I didn't want to control it. The tears started running and everything was happening to me–it was just a wonderful experience, and something I truly never expected. (Alpha News April 1994, P9)

Emotions, tears, feelings of being loved by God, these are the 'bread and butter' of the *Alpha* course.

Of course these experiences are not restricted to the 'Weekend Away'. The course is flexible and encouragement is given along the way to be 'open to God'. Here is the report from a *Youth Alpha* course leader:

We cover the talks about the Holy Spirit at the weekend, although one of the things that we've discovered is that from the word go there's such a hunger that we've been praying for the Holy Spirit to come earlier. Kids nowadays are so geared into experience that they are well open to that. (Alpha News November 1996, P9)

The experiences are imparted at many stages in *Alpha* and not exclusively at the 'Day/Weekend Away'. Wherever these experiences occur, there is no doubt that these play a significant role in supposedly confirming the reality of God to participants on the course. From *Youth Alpha* to the work in prisons, across the whole board, these sorts of phenomena and manifestations are of vital importance.

But is it the 'real thing'?

For all the sincerity of *Alpha* participants believing that they have truly met with God, we are left with a number of questions. Are these experiences comparable with what we have learnt already about the works of the Holy Spirit in bringing true repentance and faith? In all honesty, as we look at the testimonies of people and the Biblical meaning of repentance and faith, the answer has to be 'no'.

Let us recall again some of the hallmarks of repentance and faith. Is there conviction of sin? Do people experience shame for sin? Have people felt the severity of God's law and understood the justness of God's condemnation of us? Is there comprehension of the fact that God addresses us as sinners who are in danger of being eternally damned? Do people cling to Christ and Christ alone to save, the true expression of trusting faith? We look in vain for them during the 'Weekend-Away'. They are simply not there.

For example, it is difficult to equate the converting of a soul bound for hell with the experiences that we have seen above or with many others that could have been included here. For many it is simply an emotional experience or bodily sensation devoid of anything meaningful. There is no conviction of sin, no grasp of one's spiritual state, no comprehension of the holiness of God or of our desperate need to be reconciled to Him.

We have already seen that the experience of repentance and faith did not feature during the evangelistic part of the course. 'Praying the prayer' did not achieve much. It all awaits the Holy Spirit Weekend-Away to 'kick-start' the whole thing. But while this produces experiences aplenty, it does not fill in the gap and supply the missing ingredients of repentance and faith. The evangelistic part of *Alpha* failed to convert and the 'Holy Spirit Weekend-Away' does no better. At the very point where *Alpha* appears to succeed as an effective evangelistic tool, it fails utterly. It would be an understatement to say that this is very disturbing.

Phenomenal success?

What then can be said about the experiences that people have when they shake or cry or feel burning sensations? Are these the work of the Holy Spirit? Are people being introduced to the person of the Holy Spirit as those who are on the 'Weekend-Away' are promised?

The experiences which people have are not surprising since they have already been led to expect such things. That much is clear. It is also evident that people often find something 'happening to them' as if it were beyond their control. What is perhaps less clear to many is that these experiences, far from being the work of the Holy Spirit, can be achieved by anybody entering into an 'altered state of consciousness'. All the instructions that are given to people are preparations for going into a state of consciousness where the normal thought processes are stopped and the mind, at least to some extent, disabled. This is abundantly plain from the teaching about speaking in tongues. We are told to start speaking in any language as long as it is not English or any other language that we know. It is something that is conducted outside of the orbit of the rational mind. When in this state of mind, it is astonishing what can happen and what the human body is capable of feeling. Unfortunately it has nothing to do with the Spirit of God.

Consider for a moment some of the things which happen to people.

Apart from the tongues, there are various emotional feelings, burning sensations, tinglings and other manifestations. The list of possibilities has grown considerably with the arrival of the 'Toronto Blessing' which has added a new repertoire that includes animal noises and production-line 'slaying in the Spirit'. Anything can and does happen.

Space does not permit us here to examine fully the inadequacy of charismatic theology and apologists for phenomena. Others have done this extensively. (See for example, Masters and Whitcomb 1992; Wright 1996; MacArthur 1992; Glover *et al* 1997). Yet it may come as a surprise to supporters of *Alpha* as well as 'signs and wonders' generally that these phenomena are available to people of all faiths and none. One non-Christian 'healer' tells of his own experience in these words:

The patient will sometimes sense the healing begin even before I have stood up, demonstrating that the power comes from beyond the healer and is simply directed through him. I have already slipped into what has been called 'the Alpha state', which is an extra state of tranquillity. I then get out of my chair and place my hands very gently on the shoulders of the patient, eventually moving to the head and then slowly down the spine—the spinal cord is an extension of the brain. The healing process is very quiet and gentle. The patient may or may not feel some of what I feel—a tingling, or heat or cold. It makes my hands shake slightly and the heat or cold does not always relate to the actual temperature of my hands. (Edwardes 1994, P32)

We need not make too much of the unfortunate reference to the 'Alpha state' as having anything to do with the *Alpha* course but the feelings and sensations listed most certainly do. These are exactly the phenomena that Gumbel prepares participants on the 'Weekend-Away' to receive.

Here is the report of one of Edwardes' 'patients':

In the healing room, Phil told me to clear my mind, so I concentrated on the bowl of roses on the window sill in front of me. He put on some very soothing classical music, which I loved, so I found it quite easy to relax. He put his hands first on my shoulders, then on my head. I had the sensation of everything just dropping away—the pain, tension, everything—all falling away under his hands. There was a tingling coming from his hands too. I remember feeling very, very cold afterwards. As soon as I got home I fell into a dead sleep for two hours. (Edwardes 1994, P60)

Sensations, tinglings, these are all part of *Alpha* as well. The same relaxed 'altered state of consciousness', the same results, but in the case of Edwardes from a man who explicitly denies the God of the Scriptures.

As a final example of one of Edwardes' healings, one woman relates:

I have always been a tense, anxious person and when I first sat on that stool I felt more nervous than ever. Then Phil put on some music and I began to relax. Suddenly I felt what I can only describe as a rectangle of heat in my back—and this was before he had touched me. It was like a mild electric shock. I was embarrassed to find myself crying, but I could not help it. I just felt an overwhelming sense of peace sitting there. (Edwardes 1994, P44)

The comparisons with the Holy Spirit 'Weekend-Away' are too striking to miss. People being overwhelmed with feelings, crying and not understanding why, tinglings, electric shocks and sensations, this is identical to what happens on the *Alpha* course. The only difference is that *Alpha* attributes these things to the Holy Spirit rather than some impersonal force. Put bluntly, these are not genuine spiritual experiences. They are brought about by inducing people into a highly emotional state where they lose self-control.

Manuals on self-hypnotism teem with examples like this. Non-Christian hypnotist Ronald Shone, writing on the subject of hypnotism, tells us what to expect when entering into an 'altered state of consciousness' where our mind is switched off:

Once relaxation is achieved, if not before, you may experience a tingling sensation, especially in the legs and feet...These reactions are quite normal and can give the feeling of vitality. (Shone 1982, P68)

Elsewhere he tells us:

...you may feel a tingling sensation throughout parts of your body—almost as if you can feel an exchange of energy taking place... (Shone 1982, P45)

The *Alpha* course has merely succeeded in introducing people to hypnotism in a major way. Its experiences belong for the most part to the province of the flesh and have nothing to do with bringing us closer to God or communicating information about Him to us. These contrast strongly with the frame of mind in which God deals with sinners–namely when they are wide-awake. That was certainly the experience of those listening to Peter's sermon on the Day of Pentecost. They were 'cut to the heart' (Acts 2:37), not 'tingling all over'.

It is no surprise then to find such phenomena occurring in false religions: Kundalini yoga is especially adept in producing such things. In a quotation from the Grofs, who have written on the subject of this practice, we discover:

...individuals involved in this process might find it difficult to control their behaviour; during powerful rushes of Kundalini energy, they often emit various involuntary sounds and their bodies move in strange and unexpected patterns. Among the most common manifestations...are unmotivated and unnatural laughter or crying, talking tongues...and imitating a variety of animal sounds and movements. (Grof in 'Focus' Winter 1994/5, P5)

Given the identical nature of the phenomena of *Alpha* and the 'Toronto Blessing' with the New Age and false religion, it comes as no surprise to find that these methods and experiences are entirely absent from the pages of Scripture. Does Paul use them in Athens? Or in Lystra? Or does Peter employ them on the Day of Pentecost in Jerusalem? No. They are totally and utterly absent. The word of God is preached. Hearers are 'cut to the heart'. No tingling, no sensations, no laughing, no falling over. The whole atmosphere is different. *Alpha* has missed its way entirely in promoting these phenomena as part of its course.

But Jesus loves me doesn't he?

Aside from the phenomena themselves, people also claim to feel the love of God. The experience received as part of the teaching on the Holy Spirit often engenders an experience of being loved, of being a special person, as the testimonies we reported earlier bear out. Another woman who attended the course found something similar:

I saw this incredible white light and my whole body, from my head to my toes, was bathed with bright white light. Liquid love was flooding into me and I kept saying over and over again, "I've met Jesus, I've met Jesus!" (Alpha News March 1998, P13)

The fact, however, that these experiences are generated when in a state of mind not sanctioned by the Bible, immediately puts us on the alert. What emerges is that the love, although felt and thought to be real, has no real biblical context. It is not grounded in the fact that love is displayed to wicked sinners who fully deserve God's wrath. It is not communicated in a form that relates it to the work of Christ to save sinners. Neither is it the result of assurance from having put our faith in Christ. Instead, there appears to be a mysterious work of assurance that takes place before there has been anything resembling repentance and faith. The 'love' often comes as a bolt out of the blue and often in the absence of anything connecting with the need for forgiveness or the sense of needing to flee from the wrath to come. It is much gentler and cosier than that.

Indeed often it is more like a Jesus who makes light of sin and simply wants to affirm to the person that they are loved. It is a communication of unconditional acceptance rather than an indication of the huge cost to the Son of God in procuring salvation from sin. Sometimes it is coupled to a feeling that we are 'special' to God rather than fit for condemnation. Indeed there is frequently a belief that Jesus has been with us throughout our lives wanting to love us. It was there in the testimony of Wimber recounted earlier:

Suddenly I knew something that I had never known before; I had hurt God's feelings. He loved me and in his love for me he sent Jesus. But I had turned away from that love; I had shunned it all of my life. (Wimber in Gumbel 1997b, P53)

Paul in Athens tells his hearers that God had overlooked '...*times of ignorance...*' (*Acts 17:30*) on the part of sinners before they came to faith in him. It is not that we have simply failed to know how much love God was showing us. It was that we were utterly ignorant of his ways and how to worship Him. He was patiently bearing with us although we were provoking him to his face by our attitudes and behaviour. But *Alpha* starts with us and our problems rather than the holy character of God and so it is not a surprise to find that God's love collapses into showing us how special we always were to him.

Harking back briefly to the writings of Phil Edwardes, the non-Christian 'healer', it is interesting to find an echo of this:

There is nothing wrong with you for, as distinct from your body, you are totally special. You started out totally special. You can't improve on 'totally special'. You can ignore it, or lose sight of it, but you can't lose it. (Edwardes 1994, P67 Emphasis in original)

It is curious that *Alpha* is passing on the same message to some of its participants as a non-Christian healer tells his clients.

Back to the past

Many people who find their way on the *Alpha* course have come to their wits' end. There are a number of harrowing stories that are told about the failures of marriages, about futile and damaging excursions into alcohol and drug abuse, of sicknesses and sadnesses. Frequently, *Alpha* has provided a happy ending to what has undoubtedly been a period of terrible trauma. Time and time again, there is a lengthy description of breakdowns in family life, fruitless searches for meaning, hardships and problems. The stories are real and gripping. They show the real stuff of life.

Similarly there are frank accounts of wrong choices that had been made, of anti-social behaviour. Many of the people who go on *Alpha* have 'lived a bit' and been around long enough to have made mistakes in relationships, in career choices or to have endured considerable mental or physical suffering. Often it is at the 'Weekend Away' that matters come to a head and that things begin to get sorted out.

Yet, while sympathy is in order for undoubted suffering and hardship, the whole process is more often than not 'me-centred' rather than 'God-centred'. The 'Jesus' of *Alpha* comes to give pain relief rather than conversion. It is often therapy and 'healing' he brings, rather than a deep sense of conviction for sin. This again is worrying. Ultimately it can be traced back to the approach which is taken right from the outset with *Alpha*. It is an 'us-centred' course. It begins with our largely existential problems and how God can help us in the dark, confused, and lost world that we inhabit. For sure, we are told that He died for our sins, but we have already seen that the treatment of sin is superficial. God is there essentially to make life better for us. And this is precisely what *Alpha* achieves: people's experiences show a God who comes to repair damaged and hurting people rather than to reveal to them that they are 'sinners in the hands of an angry God'. For all the sympathy that the Lord shows for us and for all the tenderness that he displays to us as he rebuilds us, we are '...*by nature children of wrath, just as the others.' (Ephesians 2:3)*. Far from being invisibly loved by a God who is always 'there for us' we are the objects of God's displeasure.

He who believes in the Son has everlasting life; and he who does not believe the Son shall not see life, but the wrath of God abides on him. (John 3:36).

This is a far less palatable alternative than *Alpha* gives to us. The apostle Paul, reflecting upon a life-time of religion before he was converted, can find little that he wants to say about it. He writes:

Yet indeed I also count all things loss for the excellence of the knowledge of Christ Jesus my Lord, for whom I have suffered the loss of all things, and count them as rubbish, that I may gain Christ...(Philippians 3:8)

It is strong language. He has no enduring fascination with himself or with his past life. The past life is as 'rubbish' to him. He had acted '...*igno-rantly in unbelief...' (1 Timothy 1:13)*. His experience of God's love toward him was not of a sentimental God who was 'there for him' but of a God who showed him 'mercy' (*1 Timothy 1:13*).

Too many experiences on *Alpha*, especially but not exclusively at the 'Weekend-Away', have a God who rescues us from sadness rather than sin.

It is a gentler treatment that people find on the *Alpha* course than the Bible would allow.

They were a nice group of people

This impression is only further enhanced by hearing some of the experiences of people who were deeply moved by the love which they felt on the course from the people whom they met. These included both course leaders and small-group discussion leaders, as well as the other participants on *Alpha*. As an example, one woman writes of her experiences:

I felt a little apprehensive at first because I knew there would be many people there whom I had never met before. I should not have worried–I was greeted at the door with a wonderful welcome. At no point was I left alone or feeling out of place...Now I know why I was shown so much love from people at the Alpha course. It was the Lord's love working through them... (Alpha News December 1995, P23)

Now of course it is right for the Lord's people to be welcoming and loving. This is to be a hallmark of their behaviour. Christians are to '*...adorn the doctrine of God our Saviour in all things.' (Titus 2:10)*. People can indeed adorn the doctrine of God. But they are not a substitute for it. With *Alpha,* with its emphasis on small-groups, 'sharing times', fun, sympathy and understanding, there is a danger of being converted to a loving group of people rather than to God himself. Having found in a world of misery and darkness a group of people whom we have come to appreciate and who have shown genuine interest in and concern for us, we may uncritically and unthinkingly embrace their God as our God. Here is another example. A woman who attended *Alpha* relates her own experience of the course:

The question I wanted answered was, "Why was everyone at St John's being so nice to me?" They didn't know me, so what possible reason did they have to show me such care and compassion?...I was, week by week, enchanted by the enthusiasm, skill and cheerfulness of the cooks and backroom helpers. As the course progressed I thought, "Wow. Whatever it is that these people are 'on', I want to be on it too." (Alpha News July 1996, P4)

Of course, nobody would want to say that Christians in their evangelism should be unfriendly or hostile but *Alpha's* warm acceptance and easy-going feel risk making the atmosphere that it generates a substitute for the gospel itself. Something is being believed because a group of loving and generous people happen to believe in it. If they happened to believe in something completely different, it is possible that this 'god' would be equally acceptable. It is the message itself which should do the converting rather than the love of the people on the course.

Time spent together especially on the 'Weekend Away' and on other 'Days Away' cements relationships, but also brings emotional pressure to commit oneself to something not properly understood. The reasons have less to do with the person of Christ and more to do with wanting to belong to the group. Some church leaders talk about the 'addiction' which people have to *Alpha* because of the relationships which are generated, both among the leaders and the participants. One church leader comments:

So many people were hooked on our first Alpha course that they were showing withdrawal symptoms as the completion of the first course approached. (Alpha News July 1996, P13)

Obviously the language is exaggerated but the need to disentangle true faith and real repentance from a desire to conform to the belief-system of a likeable group of people is very real. It would not be such a problem if there were adequate systems in place to detect such false conversions or proper training of leaders to be able to detect if repentance and faith were absent but as we have already seen, these things are not present.

A life-changing experience?

Many who attend *Alpha* report that they have turned out better people than when they started the course. There has been 'value-added' through attending the course. Divorces that were imminent prior to *Alpha* were then prevented by going on the *Alpha* course (*Alpha News* July 1996, P35). There are people now better able to cope with their disabilities (*Alpha News* December 1995, P24). A wife reports of her husband who attended *Alpha*:

Overnight, my husband's personality changed–the hardness and aggression seemed to have gone and he seemed calmer. I kept telling myself it was too good to be true. (Alpha News July 1997, P5)

Marriages have been enriched, families reconciled, even reports of healing have been surfacing (*Alpha News* July 1997:5). Here is the example of one man whose behaviour certainly changed. After hearing one of the talks, he knew that there were things that were wrong in his life:

At the end of the talk, the Holy Spirit was invited to come and I felt a really intense glowing sensation. At the point of repentance I got a series of images in my mind about the things that were wrong in my life which I had to put right before I could fully become a Christian and accept the gospel. And I repented of all of them. I felt I had been forgiven for everything I'd ever done in the past–a total release from all my burdens. It made me break down and I sat down and cried...I followed the prayer Nicky suggested word for word. I thanked God for his son Jesus Christ; I repented of everything in the past; I asked for forgiveness and invited Jesus Christ into my life. I finally knew that I was a Christian...I came home after church on the Sunday night of that same weekend and I started throwing out everything that I could find that connected me in any way with the Tarot business...In fact, I have sorted out everything from that sequence of visions and I'm much happier for it. The Lord is totally in control now. (In Elsdon-Dew (ed) 1995, P80)

Neither is there any reason for people to be sceptical that these things will not last. The benefits may well be long-lasting and of great help to those who have experienced them.

Yet it is worrying again that this 'repentance' was produced after one of the 'Holy Spirit' experiences. We have already established that these do not come from God. People are not on safe ground to draw spiritual conclusions about their state of acceptance before God when influenced by manifestations and phenomena of this sort. Sometimes, in the context of an 'altered state of consciousness' people say that they simply 'know' they are forgiven. But on what basis do people 'know'? A 'sequence of visions'? A 'word of prophecy' or encouragement believed to have come from God? Experiences of being 'forgiven' induced when in a state of mind which is outside that permitted in Scripture have no place in the God-ordained means for our salvation. Faith does not come by having a vision, or an experience that confirms to us that we are forgiven. It comes through hearing the preached word of God (*Romans 10:14*). That is the God-appointed means. No other way is given to us in Scripture. *Alpha's* method is utterly unbiblical.

We need to remember it is not the exclusive preserve of the Christian faith to be able to change people's lives for the better. All religions have their testimonies of people who changed for the better as a result of their encounter with their particular faith. New Age practices can induce behavioural change in people. Hypnotherapy and self-hypnosis have their success stories.

It was evident to the Puritans that there could be significant changes in the life-style and behaviour of a person without there having been necessarily genuine conversion. They were very careful to distinguish among the different cases that presented themselves. Thomas Watson recognised the existence of such possibilities. Among his categories of counterfeit repentance he noted that:

A sin may be left not so much from strength of grace as from reasons of prudence. A man sees that though such a sin be for his pleasure, yet it is not for his interest. It will eclipse his credit, prejudice his health, impair his estate. Therefore, for prudential reasons, he dismisses it. True leaving of sin is when the acts of sin cease from the infusion of a principle of grace, as the air ceases to be dark from the infusion of light. (Watson 1987, P16-17)

Moral reform is not enough if it is not grounded upon a genuine work of the Holy Spirit, an 'infusion of grace'. Vaughan wrote astutely on the subject when observing that there were distinctions to be made in what is true and what is false or natural conviction of sin.

The natural conviction is confined almost entirely to outward actions, and these the specific actions which it has come to dread for their dangerous consequences upon the interests of this life. It has no reference to the great fountain head of sin, the unholy heart, and the inward sinfulness determined by it. (Vaughan 1975, P70)

Of course there are examples of people parting with their bad habits and becoming better people. Some people list the sins and the broken relationships they painfully put right. But there is little evidence of people realising that they are sinners before God and have offended His law, a point we have returned to on more than one occasion. It is not enough to stop doing certain 'bad things' or even of 'putting some things right'. Repentance is brought about through realising that we are helpless sinners who are deserving of the wrath of God. If course participants are crying out 'What must I do to be saved?', it is *Alpha's* best kept secret.

It is time to conclude this section. We have seen the important part that experiences play in leading people to conclude that God is real. The 'Weekend Away' occupies a key position in this although the course allows for opportunities all along the way for such experiences to be generated. It is to be feared that many of these experiences are not genuine but are induced through an 'altered state of consciousness'.

We can go further, in fact. The evangelistic component falls largely flat as 'nothing' happens. The 'Holy Spirit Weekend Away' misses the mark because the 'wrong thing' happens. While supplying the missing experiential component from the evangelistic section, it substitutes a false experience. It is not the Holy Spirit who is 'introduced' to people on the 'Weekend-Away'. Having failed to encounter Christ in their mechanical 'praying of a prayer', they then fail again to encounter Him on the 'Weekend-Away'. The 'love of God' is not grasped in its Biblical context but is often replaced by the unconditional love of a God who is 'always there for me'. Conversion is more a matter of finding a new meaning to life rather than fleeing to Christ to *'Be saved from this perverse generation.' (Acts 2:40).*

At the risk of repetition, we can see that a whole family of problems stem from the fact that *Alpha* has not presented a Biblical portrait of God or man. It fails to offer a meaningful gospel but has simply set forth a loving God whom we are invited to believe in without any proper explanation of what He is like or what He requires of man. The testimonies of people doing the course bear this out. The very success claimed for *Alpha* as a great evangelistic tool proves in the end to be hollow.

A very broad church

Our examination of *Alpha* is nearly complete. We have seen that it does not preach the Biblical gospel. It does not appeal to us on the basis of the need to repent and believe, but more on the basis of vague and sentimental love. The 'Weekend Away' fails to remedy the situation despite all that is claimed for it.

This begs some very important questions. The most basic is–does *Alpha* actually understand what a Christian is? Having failed to grasp the gospel and the meaning of repentance and faith, does it basically misunderstand what a Christian is? The answer as we shall see in this brief chapter is 'yes'. *Alpha's* notion of what constitutes a Christian and a Christian church is very wide.

A cast of thousands

One thing *Alpha* is not short of is quotations from different authorities and experts. Some of these are very helpful. Quotations and allusions to people like J.C. Ryle (Gumbel 1997B, P46) and Puritan Thomas Goodwin (Gumbel 1997B, P157) are very welcome. Other references are not so helpful and betray the disastrously wide understanding that *Alpha* has of what constitutes a Christian.

For example, Paul Tillich, is held up as a '*...theologian and philosopher...*' *(Gumbel 1997b, P22)*. This is a liberal thinker who can scarcely be claimed as an evangelical. The German theologian Jürgen Moltmann is another liberal (Gumbel 1997B, P49). He too is quoted approvingly and uncritically. Representatives of Roman Catholicism, a body that denies fundamental doctrines about the gospel and Biblical truth, are also permitted to speak through the medium of *Alpha*. Evangelicals are hardly likely to draw the same comfort as Gumbel evidently does from the fact that Vatican II claims to hold a high view of the inspiration of Scripture (Gumbel 1997B, P76). *Alpha* has no difficulty quoting with approval Tom Forrest, a Roman Catholic (Gumbel 1997B, P185). Mother Teresa is accepted as a Christian despite evidence that she held no firm Christian convictions (Gumbel 1997B, P190). At another place it is the Pope's personal preacher whose words we are hearing (Gumbel 1997B, P227).

We do not have to make a judgement about the spiritual standing of these people, but it is evident that they represent in their teachings and church adherence, positions that are diametrically opposed to the gospel as it has been laid out in this book. True evangelicalism has no place for salvation through sacraments, the intercessory and mediatory work of Mary or the existence of purgatory after this life. Many central teachings of the Roman Catholic Church are nowhere to be found in Scripture and are in fact directly opposed to the work of Christ. They are not minor aberrations but fundamental departures from the historic Christian faith. Yet *Alpha* quotes from its spokespeople and representatives uncritically. There is not a murmur of reservation, not a hint of a doctrinal quibble.

Since *Alpha* purports to help those who are just starting out in the Christian faith, such a loose approach is nothing short of irresponsible. It takes no genius to see that the potential for confusion is enormous. No warnings are given to us that these people represent fundamentally unsound churches or theological views. The young believer whom *Alpha* claims to be helping is left to find out the hard way. They are given a confusing message which will be of no help to them as they seek to find their way in the Christian life and attempt to understand and evaluate the different views to which they will be exposed.

Any church will do...

This cavalier attitude extends to the recommendation of churches that *Alpha* feels happy to give. If we are evangelicals we are not likely to be thrilled by Gumbel's advice that:

In one sense it is not so important what denomination we are—Roman Catholic or Protestant; Lutheran, Methodist, Baptist, Pentecostal, Anglican or House Church. What is more important is whether or not we have the Spirit of God. If people have the Spirit of God living within them, they are Christians, and our brothers and sisters. (Gumbel 1997B, P148)

Of course there are Christians in many denominations. True believers in the Lord can be found in some of the most unlikely places. But it is plainly wrong to tell new Christians that it does not essentially matter which church they belong to. It matters greatly, because in some churches and some church denominations the true gospel and biblical teaching will not be heard. It is most irresponsible to suggest to young believers that it is virtually a matter of indifference which church they attend. *Alpha's* view of the church is far too broad.

Thank you for your support?

This same looseness surfaces in the kinds of alliances that the proponents of the *Alpha* course are seeking to make. The fact, for example, that the Roman Catholic church has so enthusiastically embraced *Alpha* is heralded by the promoters of *Alpha* as a significant development. Conferences have been held to introduce *Alpha* to the Roman Catholic community. There is now a special *Alpha* Catholic office. As reported in 1997 in *Alpha News*:

More than 450 packed into London's Westminster Cathedral Hall in May for the first Roman Catholic Alpha conference, which had been overbooked for four months. The conference which had received a message of encouragement from Cardinal Hume, the Archbishop of Westminster, was led by Sandy Millar and Nicky Gumbel, of Holy Trinity Brompton. (Alpha News July 1997, P1)

It would appear that it was very much appreciated. The report continues:

Introducing the event, Bishop Ambrose Griffiths, Roman Catholic Bishop of Hexham and Newcastle, described the Alpha course as "the most powerful evangelistic tool, which reaches out precisely to those whom we need." (Alpha News July 1997, P1)

It would appear that representatives of the Catholic Church also believe that *Alpha* 'works'. They are hoping *Alpha* will reverse the decline in its numbers especially among young people. As Bishop Griffiths conceded:

We all, as Catholics, certainly, face a great problem. We do not seem to be attracting young people or young families and meanwhile our congregations get older and fewer. This is our common experience. (Alpha News July 1997, P12)

The Roman Catholic Bishop of Leeds, the Right Rev David Konstant, has no misgivings about *Alpha*:

The Alpha course is a valuable contribution to our commitment to evangelisation as we move towards the new millennium, and I am sure it will be of great benefit to the Church's mission. (Alpha News July 1997, P3)

We should not be surprised at this support being shown for *Alpha* by the Roman Catholic Church. As we have seen, *Alpha* fails to present the gospel but substitutes a vague 'God of love' in its place. Everyone and anyone can subscribe to this deity. There is nothing to offend those who hold to another gospel than that preached by the apostles. So we find Ambrose Griffiths again saying about *Alpha*:

It is not a complete exposition of Catholic doctrine. No introductorycourse could possibly do that. But it doesn't contain anything that is Contrary to Catholic doctrine. (Alpha News July 1997, P1)

Nothing 'contrary to Catholic doctrine?'. How is this possible especially in the light of the ringing endorsements given by so many of the leading authorities of the evangelical-charismatic world? We should not wonder. *Alpha* does not preach the gospel and so has much to commend it to other agencies that do not preach it either.

Even liberals who have abandoned much of evangelical faith can find much good in *Alpha*. *Alpha News* reported a visit by the arch-liberal the Right Rev Richard Holloway, Episcopal Bishop of Edinburgh, to an *Alpha* Supper in a town in Scotland. There was no problem about advertising his presence and no apology for his liberal views. Neither it seems did he have any problem accepting the invitation. Indeed, what he had to say fitted in very well with the ethos of *Alpha*. Listen to this reported excerpt of his address:

So I pray that you who use the Alpha course—you who belong to the churches of this area—will understand in your own hearts how utterly and unconditionally you are loved by God no matter what youknow against yourself. (Alpha News July 1996, P3)

A liberal Bishop appears to have spotted what a host of evangelicals have failed to pick up. *Alpha's* gospel speaks of a God of 'unconditional love' who does not hate sin as the Bible would have us to believe. He is a more sentimental God than we find in the pages of Scripture and one with which the liberal church is more at home. Why cannot evangelicals see this?

We're all Christians now

The *Alpha* course presents then a very wide definition of the Christian church and is happy to accept plaudits from those who are by no stretch of the imagination evangelical. As we have seen in Chapter Eight, it is also happy to affirm the experiences of people who appear, from what they say, to have received something other than the Holy Spirit and to have undergone something different from Biblical repentance and faith. By this token, becoming a Christian is something infinitely easier than the narrow way suggested by the Scriptures.

Alpha's criteria of what constitutes a Christian are consequently very broad. The quotation we saw earlier makes this point. As long as we have the 'Spirit of God' we are all brothers and sisters according to *Alpha*. We can practically believe what we like. We can hold opposing and contradictory views about the message of salvation but we are 'brothers and sisters' if we have had the experience of the 'Spirit'. This is a disastrous view to hold. On the basis of a spurious experience such as mediated at the 'Weekend Away', a person is accepted as a *bona fide* Christian. The fact that all that is shared in common is the experience of an unbiblical 'altered state of consciousness' is lost on the promoters of *Alpha*. On this reading, almost half the world must be Christians! It is a faulty message. It can only heighten the problems that will be experienced in the nominally evangelical church struggling to insist upon the need for doctrine. If *Alpha's* view prevails, such an appeal will fall on increasingly deaf ears.

And then there's the 'Toronto Blessing'

Finally it is no accident that the church that has developed the *Alpha* course has been one of the foremost supporters of the so-called 'Toronto Blessing', the charismatic experience characterised by hysterical laughter, bodily sensations, involuntary collapsing to the floor, convulsions and even animal noises.

Holy Trinity, Brompton has been unapologetic in its support for the 'Toronto Blessing'. Many of the supporters and participating churches in *Alpha* are likewise sympathetic to this 'latest move of the Spirit'. There is not the space to look at this phenomenon in detail here. Others have done this at length (See Wright 1996; and Glover *et al* 1997). From what has been seen of the 'Weekend Away', it is plain that this is nothing other than a form of the 'blessing' with all its non-biblical phenomena and effects. Churches that have been able to embrace the practices of the 'Weekend Away' have quite logically been able to embrace the 'Toronto Blessing'. They are at root one and the same thing–experiences derived in an altered state of consciousness.

It comes then as no surprise that churches which are hopelessly led astray on the matter of the working of the Holy Spirit can be equally undiscerning when it comes to understanding what is the gospel. There is not the space to develop the thesis here, but the correlation between the two errors is probably very close. For both at heart are failures to understand the glory of God's holy being.

Alpha's support base is therefore very suspect. It finds encouragement from causes that oppose evangelicalism and is itself the product of a church that embraces the unbiblical phenomenon of the 'Toronto Blessing'. It is a reflection of a broad definition of what a Christian is and what the church is, and its increasing acceptance among so many churches will only serve to broaden these concepts further in the future.

Is there life after Alpha?

It has to be said that many of the criticisms that are levelled against *Alpha* are unfair. Although mostly associated with Holy Trinity Brompton in west London, it is not a middle-class phenomenon. *Alpha* 'works' in the inner city, among young people and in prisons. It is also wrong to label it a cult, as some commentators have done. Following their logic, we would probably have to conclude that every church in the land is a cult. Criticisms like these are not valid. A lot of thought and time has been put into the construction of the course. A number of genuine and sincere people are involved who have an evident desire to do some good and to be helpful.

Nothing that has been said is intended in any way to impugn the integrity of those who are running the courses or who have put the course together in the first place. Most if not all doubtless do believe very firmly that *Alpha* is working. They may well be incredulous at the criticisms which are made in this book. Neither is there any reason to minimise the apparent impact of the course on many churches. It has brought in new people and adherents. It has galvanised inward-looking churches to consider the world outside their front door. It has engendered team work and a sense of commitment to a common cause. Yet when placed against the Scriptures as to what is the gospel, and what is true repentance and faith, it flounders. It has not produced what is claimed for it and we need to be aware of this if we are tempted to use it in our own churches.

Liberalism for a new day

Essentially *Alpha's* gospel is a form of liberalism. Under cover of evangelical language a new liberalism has been emerging. Its influence has been steadily growing. Its numbers are becoming ever more significant. Confidence among its ranks is sky-high. It really believes that it has the answers for our day and age.

Bringing a message and methods that fit well with this experience-centred generation, it is attempting and nearly succeeding in sweeping all before it. It retains some of the arguments of the evangelical faith but has evacuated them of meaning. It believes in the literal person of Christ and the miracles that he performed but has no place for the holiness of God. It believes in reaching the lost but tells them a different gospel. It is full of love but has no place for telling sinners the truth. There is a belief in the Holy Spirit but no room found for the evidences of his working in true repentance and faith. It is a substitute for the real thing. Where there should be a God of glory and majesty, we have a God of sentimental and unconditional love. Where there should be a call to repentance, the new liberalism has replaced it with a call to return to the love of God. The time has come to call it for what it is–it is another God, another Jesus, and another gospel. It is not building the true church but is constructing a false one which has no appetite but only scorn for biblical truth. For evangelicals, it is no friend of ours and we should avoid it at all costs.

Some may wonder whether it is possible to use parts of the course. Unfortunately, by the time the caveats had been applied, the evangelistic material completely recast, the 'Weekend Away' radically revised, there would be little left of *Alpha*. To try to use it, having taken out all the offending parts, would be like trying to show someone London without going to the Tower of London, Trafalgar Square, Oxford Street, the Houses of Parliament or Buckingham Palace. Most of its 'highlights' would have gone. Stripped of its charismatic elements, the 'Holy Spirit Weekend Away', and its ecumenical leanings and with a totally recast evangelistic argument, it would have changed beyond recognition–and we would fall foul of copyright for all our trouble!

So what do we replace it with?

This is perhaps the obvious question to try to answer at this stage. It seems a reasonable one to pose. Many churches have cast envious glances at *Alpha*. It appears to believe all the wrong things, do all the wrong things, and yet still sees conversions. This impression causes confusion for a lot of believers. This sorry state of affairs is somewhat relieved if we take on board the argument of this book, that *Alpha* is not seeing the conversions that are claimed. For those that love the God of the Scriptures, *Alpha* is a non-starter. Yet too often the underlying problem is that people are desperate for something that will 'work', for something that will draw people into the church at the dawn of the new millennium. So what do we do if we do not have *Alpha*?

The answer is not a novel one. It is this—we need to preach the gospel. This solution is not as exasperatingly simple as it may seem at first glance. Many may feel that they have been preaching it for years without seeing any fruit. That may well be true. It is, after all, a very dark day in which God's servants are having to labour. But it may also be true that a lot of churches are not as clear in their gospel preaching as they might be.

Recalling the findings of Chapters Three and Four on the Biblical gospel there may be lessons to learn. There may not be the clarity in the message that there should be. Neither might there be the direct application that there needs to be. Finally there may not be an authentic call to true repentance and faith to complete it. Instead, churches are putting up with something less than the gospel while still believing that they are gospel churches.

This impression is given further confirmation when we remember how many professing evangelicals have shown interest in the *Alpha* course. The list of people endorsing it reads almost as a *'Who's Who?'* of the contemporary evangelical scene. Undoubtedly many of these have not properly examined the course and on closer inspection would probably prefer to revise their estimate of *Alpha*. Even allowing for this, it is still evidence of considerable confusion about what the gospel is. Many are seemingly unable to recognise whether the gospel has been preached or not. There is little discernment about whether the death of Christ is being accurately set forth. Neither is there much comprehension about the wrath of God or the need to preach the law of God.

A little truth about Jesus, and people seem to be happy that the gospel has been faithfully presented. The mere mention of sins and a gentle hint about judgement, and people are satisfied that Biblical evangelism has taken place. However, it is not enough to believe the basics about the life of Christ, or to maintain that the events, including the miracles, actually took place. There has to be more. God's holy character has to be presented. Sin in its awfulness as offence against God has to be set forth. The absolute requirement to repent and put one's faith in Christ has to be proclaimed.

These have to be preached without compromise. It is what the apostles did. It is what the early church did. It is what was recaptured during times of revival in church history. It is what is needed today.

Of course opportunities should be used to reach out to people. Events with food have their place. Small groups have a role to play. There are Bible studies that avoid the problems and present a much sounder gospel. 'For Starters' (Pond, C. 1997) is one of these and can be easily adapted for use. Another course for new believers entitled 'Starting out as a New Christian' (see below) can also be used. Meetings in different settings as well as lectures devoted to apologetics all have their place, as events at which people can ask questions and have them sympathetically and intelligently answered. (Details about Starting out as a New Christian can be obtained from: Pastor Edward Challen, 32 Dorking Road, Epsom, Surrey, KT18 7NH. UK.)

But there is no magic wand to be waved. Our task is to use the opportunities presented to us as vigorously as possible, but never to lose the true essence of the gospel which we preach. We are not at liberty to offer anything else. If the gospel, preached as carefully, prayerfully, seriously and lovingly as God enables us to preach, does not save people, we have nothing else that we can offer them. If people refuse the message of life, there is no other message that we can give them. If they cannot be brought to listen to the truth, we have no mandate to tell them something else.

However helpless we may feel in the face of such overwhelming apathy, we have no licence to produce another gospel and use something that seems to 'work'. If people will not hear the gospel, then they will not hear anything else. As the rich man, suffering the torments of hell, is told when he remonstrates about the need for signs and wonders to convince his five brothers,

If they do not hear Moses and the prophets, neither will they be persuaded though one rise from the dead. (Luke 16:31)

Somehow, the church has lost confidence in the fact that the Lord will not allow His Word to be broken. What He has said, He has meant. If, having discharged the responsibility given to us, the results are still meagre, that has to be left to the sovereignty of God. Unfortunately, in practice, there is a marked reluctance to believe in this doctrine. If the means that God has appointed are not bearing the fruit that we would desire to see, that is not the signal to change the means. Perhaps if the church was more careful and faithful in the discharge of the duties given to her, there would by now have been more to show for our efforts. Carelessness may have robbed the church of much of its blessing. God has not undertaken to bless shoddy work. While casting around to find 'something that works', we may have missed some very obvious matters closer to home that have been overlooked. Perhaps it is time to examine again the gospel that is preached and to review the evangelistic literature and methods that we employ: there may be plenty of room for improvement.

The right atmosphere?

There are a host of related issues which can only be mentioned in passing. We must, for example, examine much of what passes for worship in this day and age. Too many of the songs used in public worship lack theology and fail to describe God with the dignity proper to Him. God has been stripped of His glory in many a worship service. When this is done before unbelievers, the effects are grievous. Non-Christians witnessing God being approached in a lack-lustre, sentimental and careless way will draw their own conclusions. Songs that are shallow and more supportive of the *Alpha* God, full of sentimental love but weak on holiness and glory, will leave a lasting but wrong impression on people. Casual informality and cosy 'mateyness' with the Almighty God can work against preaching the God of the Bible and unwittingly communicate that we believe in a different God in practice. Our forebears knew more of the holiness of God than we do. We need to learn from them how they worshipped God.

Too many unbelievers are able to pass through our churches without being confronted by a God of holiness. But paradoxically, neither are they finding the biblical God of love either. We cannot meaningfully preach about the love of Christ until we have established the context of that love. It is glorious love that reaches down to poor and needy sinners who deserve nothing other than the wrath of God. Without a grasp of the holy character of God and the work that our Saviour has done in being our substitute, the love of Christ is simply incomprehensible.

Helping sinners

We are also too careless in our assessment of what are true converts. People are not being taught about Biblical repentance and faith. Instead any testimony of someone being impressed with the Christian faith is accepted as *bona fide* evidence of conversion. The true meaning of repentance as something deeper than abandoning outward practices has to be set forth. There needs to be a realisation that one is irretrievably sinful by nature. The desirability of Christ as the one to believe upon for salvation becomes clearer in the light of this. But in many evangelistic presentations the whole matter has lacked urgency and been reduced to an intellectual affirmation of basic Christian doctrines.

Looking forward

We remind ourselves that there are no easy answers to these problems. It has been evident for many years that there has not been great success for the preaching of the gospel. Desperation has led many to embrace teachings and practices that will prove at the end to have been *cul-de-sacs*. Neither Pensacola, Toronto, *Alpha* or Willow Creek supply the answers that the church is looking for. It is a symbol of how anxious many have become that some who should know better are following these routes. Disappointment can only be the end result.

Our task is to use all the strength that God has given to us and to remain faithful in the work that He has given to us to do. We are called to pray and to be diligent and such requirements we must observe carefully. It is not an hour to be faint-hearted. The task is enormous but the living God is with us. We may feel overwhelmed by the scale of the need, but God will never forsake his church '...*which He purchased with his own blood.*' *(Acts 20:28)* Though we may be yet further humbled in the future and have to endure worse apostasy still among our ranks, there can never be failure in God's work. *'I will build my church, and the gates of Hades shall not prevail against it' (Matthew 16:18)*. In the days ahead of us we may need to hold tenaciously to Scriptures such as this. Today the pressure to abandon God's appointed means in gospel work is immense. The worst, however, may be yet to come.

Alleine, J. 1989 *A Sure Guide to Heaven,* Banner of Truth, Edinburgh (first published 1671).

Chantry, W. 1989 *Today's Gospel* : Authentic or Synthetic? Banner of Truth, Edinburgh.

Edwardes, P. with De Saulles, A 1994 *Touch Them with Love,* Element, Shaftesbury.

Elsdon-Dew, M. (ed) 1995 The God Who Changes Lives, HTB Publications, London.

Glover, P et al 1997 *The Signs and Wonders Movement–Exposed,* Day One, Epsom.

Gumbel, N. 1997a *Telling Others,* Kingsway, Eastbourne.

Gumbel, N. 1997b *Questions of Life,* Kingsway, Eastbourne.

Helm, P. 1986 *The Beginnings: Word and Spirit in Conversion,* Banner of Truth, Edinburgh.

Kuiper, A. 1994 *God-Centred Evangelism,* Banner of Truth, Edinburgh (first published 1961).

MacArthur, J Jr. 1992 *Charismatic Chaos,* Zondervan, Grand Rapids.

Masters, P. and 1992 *The Charismatic Phenomenon,* Wakeman Trust, Whitcomb, J. London.

Pond, C. 1997 *For Starters,* Evangelical Press, Darlington.

Shone, R. 1987 Autohypnosis *: A Step-by-step Guide to Self-Hypnosis,* Thorsons, London.

Vaughan, C. 1994 *The Gifts of the Holy Spirit,* Banner of Truth, Edinburgh. (First published 1894).

Watson, T. 1994 *The Doctrine of Repentance,* Banner of Truth, Edinburgh (first published 1668)

Wright, E. 1996 Strange Fire?: *Assessing the Vineyard Movement and the Toronto Blessing,* Evangelical Press, Darlington.

Alpha News is produced by Holy Trinity Brompton, London.
Focus is produced by Focus Christian Ministries Trust, Lewes.

Also from Day One

The Great Exchange:
Justification by faith alone in the
light of recent thought

Philip Eveson

Philip Eveson examines the biblical evidence for justification by faith alone, presents the evangelical teaching of the Reformers and their successors, and demonstrates from its modern catechism where the Roman Catholic Church stands on the subject. At the same time, he seeks to show the relevance of justification in today's world.
Philip Eveson also answers those who deny there is a biblical doctrine of justification and no longer regard it as of central importance to the gospel and the church. The Great Exchange is an important addition to the current debate.

Paperback 228 pages   £7.99

ISBN 0 902548 73 5

For further information about other Day One titles, call or write to us:

01372 728 300

In Europe: ++ 44 1372 728 300

In North America: 011 44 1372 728 300

Day One 3 Epsom Business Park Kiln Lane Epsom Surrey KT17 1JF England

E Mail: ldos.dayone@ukonline.co.uk